scm centrebooks

D. W. D. Shaw

Who is God?

SCM PRESS LTD

SBN 334 01788 2

First published 1968
by SCM Press Ltd
56 Bloomsbury Street London WC1

© *SCM Press Ltd 1968*

Printed in Great Britain by
Billing & Sons Limited
Guildford and London

Contents

37327

Foreword

This little book has been written with a reader in mind who is intelligent but untrained in theology or philosophy. Technical terms have been kept to a minimum and, where they have been unavoidable, an attempt has been made to explain them in a non-technical way. I have also numbered paragraphs, to make the progress of the argument clearer. I hope that this course may provide some pointers in intelligible language towards an answer to the question which forms the title.

No great originality is claimed. Indeed, all the ideas expressed here owe their origin to one or other of the great thinkers of our time, whose labours have made theology such an exciting business. In order to avoid lengthy quotations and numerous footnotes, arguments and points of view under discussion are presented in general terms without specific attributions or acknowledgment. This is a dangerous proceeding, but in the circumstances it seemed to be justified. Of course I take full responsibility for everything that is said here, but I should like to acknowledge that for many of the ideas, particularly in Chapters 2 and 5, I am indebted to John McIntyre, Professor of Divinity, Philosophy of Religion and Apologetics at the University of Edinburgh, under whom I was fortunate enough to study and with whom I am privileged to teach.

Edinburgh
July 1968

1 Problem and Task

1. 'Who is God?' For many people, the title of this book will be a prime example of begging the real question by posing a bogus one. They would want to put the real question equally briefly, but rather differently: 'Is there God?' This, they feel, is the question that logically needs to be answered before going on, if necessary, to ask the further question, 'Who?' The question 'Who is God?' acquires interest and meaning for them only after it has been established to their satisfaction *that* there is a God. That 'someone did it' is, after all, assumed in any question of 'who dunnit'. The question of identification seems to presuppose the question of existence: it becomes superfluous if the prior question is not answered satisfactorily.

All this seems reasonable enough. So it is necessary to begin by saying why a rather different course is being adopted in this book.

2.1 For one thing, the more obvious approach has been tried and generally found wanting, or at least not convincing. For many centuries – it is usually St Thomas Aquinas who gets the credit or the blame – it was almost standard practice, and indeed modern examples are not hard to find. The argument started off by appealing to common sense in a variety of ways to show that the world and everything in it is not self-explanatory. Everything is dependent on something else to bring it into existence, to let it be the way it is and to let it change and cease to be. For it to have got going in the first place, to be kept going, and in a certain ordered direction too, the existence of something else behind, giving a purpose, supplying direction and meaning, was clearly thought to be required. Design in nature implied some Designer – and it is worth noting that those to whom this argument appealed were the real scientists of their day, for whom the investigation of plants, and biology and astronomy, was something of intense interest and concern, not the preoccupation of a few experts as it is now.

Or it seemed common sense that some things were good and others bad, some things right and others wrong. If such things were too obvious to be doubted, was it not simply reasonable to ask: if these values are indisputable, whence came they? And the not unreasonable answer was, 'From some supreme evaluation', which implied a Valuator. Having then established satisfactorily that the way things were in the world demanded the existence of a first principle, a mover to get things started, a supreme maintenance-man to keep things going, a valuator to give things worth, some supreme existence to give existence to everything that is, what more natural than that these should all be joined together in one supreme Being – 'and this all men call God'? This 'first principle God' must then exist. 'Is there a God?' had been satisfactorily answered and it was then pertinent to ask, 'What?'

2.2 Again reason came to the rescue. In the world as it is, with values and hopes and progress as they are, this 'first principle God' could be described in a number of ways, mainly by contrast with the human condition: in-finite, im-mutable, im-material; or spirit as opposed to matter, eternal as opposed to temporal, and so on. But reason also demanded that certain desirable human qualities should be ascribed to this 'first principle God', and he thus picked up 'supreme wisdom', 'justice', 'goodness', 'power' and such noble attributes as 'omnipotence', 'omniscience', 'omni-presence'. To do this, however, was in fact to go beyond the terms of the argument, for the argument was applicable only to the demonstration of a 'What', not a 'Who'. To arrive at the 'Who', the God of Christian theism, a further step was still necessary. The gap between the 'What' and the 'Who' was therefore bridged by the appeal to 'divine revelation', knowledge imparted by God himself through Jesus Christ, not accessible to reason alone. This was the means of conveying that God is not after all a 'thing'-like substance, however supreme, but 'personal', not a 'What', but a 'Who'.

2.3   That this kind of approach no longer carries conviction in our day needs only to be stated. Argument is unnecessary. Indeed, so alien is it to the thinking of many believers and all unbelievers that it is very difficult to do justice to it. Yet the men who propounded it and the men who accepted it were not fools: they were neither mad nor naïve. The truth is that men's thinking as well as their behaviour, their pleasures and their dress, all take place against a background of 'conventional wisdom' which has to be taken account of if their thinking is to make any sense at all. The assumptions of the age of natural theology, as it is called, were no less and no more reasonable than the assumptions or conventional wisdom of any subsequent age, including our own. To the people who propounded and accepted that kind of reasoning, the assumptions of the secular society would have made even less sense. If they had read a modern philosopher's criticism of their arguments, and seen in black and white the statements of our modern champions of self-evident atheism – the preconception that the universe is everything that is, 'the universe itself is ultimate', 'the principles of the world lie themselves inside the world' – they just could not have understood. They reasoned differently, they felt differently, they were not on the same wavelength. For this very reason, when we try to follow their procedure of moving from the existence of God to what God must be and then to 'who' he is, we fail to understand them, and no amount of frequency modulation or adjusting of receiving sets can help. This is the main reason why we eschew the 'that-what-who' procedure.

3.   But to arrive at a satisfactory alternative procedure is no easy matter. It is one thing to see what fails to carry weight or 'click' in modern minds: it is quite another to see what succeeds. The fact is that some of the most powerful

11

movements of our time, and theological movements at that, have a built-in reluctance to attempting a straight answer to the question 'Who is God?' It is worth considering briefly why this should be so. We can usefully start by asking: is there such a thing as objective knowledge of God?

3.1 It may come as a surprise to some readers to learn that many theologians today would have no hesitation in answering that question in the negative. There is no such thing as objective knowledge of God. This may sound strange, so it had better be added at once that these same theologians, while denying the possibility of objective knowledge of God, are by no means denying the possibility of knowledge of God that can be trusted and relied on and accepted as true. What they are really saying is that God is not and cannot be the subject of scientific enquiry. The scientist observes the object of his interest – the chemical substance, the plant, the star – studying every aspect of it with his microscope or telescope or whatever. He then poses a prediction or hypothesis regarding the reaction of what he is studying in certain new circumstances, and devises experiments which will show if his prediction or hypothesis is correct: if it is not, he will try again with a different hypothesis or a different experiment; if it is successful, he has discovered something true about what he is studying. New knowledge, and true knowledge, comes by observing, testing, predicting and devising convincing means of checking. That is how objective knowledge is arrived at.

3.2 It does not require a great deal of reflection to see that knowledge of that kind, scientific knowledge, 'objective' knowledge, is not the only kind of knowledge that is available to us. There are other kinds of knowledge, essential to life, where there can be no question of the laboratory approach – the white coat, the detachment, the observation, the devising and correcting of tests, the feeding of results into computers, the dispassionate writing-up and analysis of the findings. The poet, the playwright, the artist know something, have something true to say. But it would be absurd if we were to expect them to adopt the procedure of the scientist – detached, impartial observation, reported and checked. The whole point is that the artist is generally trying to say something important and true about an aspect of life, human or natural, which is precisely not amenable to the microscope or to scientific analysis. The subject involves a mystery of one kind or another, the mystery of why people act and react as they do, the mystery of persons in relation with other persons, the mystery of personal life. And in investigating this subject, the artist has to rely not only on observation, but on his intuition, on his own particular perspective, on the way in which he sees himself involved in the very situation he is seeking to study – not outside it, as the observing scientist would be, but inside it, participating in it. In other words, with the kind of truth the artist is trying to express, there is no question of his abstracting himself and claiming to present the 'objective facts'. On the contrary, the truth-content of his production will rather depend on the extent to which his creation reflects himself, his subjective contribution. Objectivity, then, is neither desirable nor possible here.

3.3 This distinction between the 'objective' truth of the scientist and the 'non-objective' truth of the artist – it is perhaps as well to avoid the word 'subjective' here, as in common parlance its overtones of 'illusion' or even 'delusion' are unfortunately too strong – is one to which theologians in our day especially are extraordinarily sensitive. They have realized that in speaking about God they are not speaking of someone or something which can be observed at a distance, experimented with, analysed in detachment, described in a neutral way. Rather, they see that their task of saying something useful and true about God requires them to be as much artists as scientists. To speak about God is to speak about something or someone who is concerned not with some aspect of existence, or part of reality, or compartment of life or nature, but with the whole of reality, the whole of the universe, the whole of life – and, therefore, the whole of man himself. There can be no separation of a man's understanding of God from his way of looking at the world, his attitude to life, and therefore his way of understanding himself. No man can understand anything about God if he does not in some way know that he is directly involved himself, with his perspectives and ambitions as well as his brain. As in the case of the 'truth' of the artist, so when we are talking about God, 'neutral' or 'objective' knowledge which does not affect our understanding of the world is neither possible nor desirable.

3.3.1 This insight into the 'non-objective' nature of knowledge of God has been one of the dominant features of theology in our time and it is one that we ignore at our peril. It has many consequences, two of which are worth mentioning at this point. The first is the impossibility of describing God in any simple, 'objective-looking' if not 'objective-meaning' formula. A contemporary Dutch philosopher looks at the question 'What is a god?' and comments, 'That's an interesting subject for a book!'[1] The framers of the Westminster Shorter Catechism (1648), memorized with exactitude and mixed feelings by generation after generation of Reformed children ever since, did not share his reserve. 'What is God?', runs Question no. 4 ('What', note, not 'Who'). The answer is short and apparently unambiguous: 'God is a Spirit, infinite, eternal and unchangeable, in his being, wisdom, power, holiness, justice, goodness and truth.' Now it would be blatantly unjust to the framers of the Shorter Catechism to imply that they expected this answer to be understood on its own, divorced from a whole complex of statements and definitions which it presupposed and which would subsequently be understood by the catechist. The fact remains that, as framed, the question seems to ask for the definition of some *thing*, a definition which the answer seems to provide, a thing, moreover, which can be described objectively, in complete isolation from the questioner or the answerer, remote enough, mysterious enough in terms of the definition, but still neutral. It may well be that the framers of the Catechism did not intend that this should be so; it may also be that for many years those who, as taught by the Catechism, used this kind of language, were able to do so without thinking of God as some object, an alien thing. But the fact is that now, conditioned, if not dominated, as we are by scientific ways of describing and thinking, a description in terms of the Shorter Catechism answer to the question 'What is God?' is bound to suggest to us that God is precisely that kind of thing which he is not – one object, albeit the greatest, among other objects of our knowledge.

3.3.2 This brings us to the second consequence of our insight concerning 'no objective knowledge of God'. This is that many theologians have been so struck by it that they now feel that virtually nothing at all can be said about God 'as he is in himself'. One school, who have been trying to re-cast the language of theology following the lead of Rudolf Bultmann, and whom we shall call *existentialists*, are so conscious of the fact that there can be no knowledge of God that does not entail knowledge of ourselves that they feel unable, in their statements about God, to go beyond statements about ourselves and our understanding of our world. For them, all that can be said about God is that he (why not it?) comes to us 'from beyond', 'encounters' us in his act, that is, in the event Jesus Christ, that on the basis and in the light of this encounter, he gives us a new understanding of ourselves, as judged and as forgiven, making us free for our neighbour and open to the future. All this we may say, and there is indeed much more to be said of the structures, possibilities and hopes of the life of faith. But to say anything relevant or true about him who comes 'from beyond', who does the encountering, who makes possible this new understanding and life of faith, about God 'as he is in himself' in contrast to God 'in his action for us', is out of the question, as it must involve a return to 'objectifying', a 'thing-making' treatment of God which must be false.

3.3.3 Yet another school, which we shall refer to as *empiricists*, takes the further step of proceeding on the basis that 'non-objective' talk of God is no more meaningful in our age than 'objective' talk about God; it has no 'cash value'; it does not 'gell'. If God cannot be spoken of objectively, then he had better not be spoken of at all. It is not for us to comment here on the intriguing 'Death of God' movement in 'theology' (that word is retained) except to say that those presently preoccupied with the 'Death of God' still spend a great deal of time discussing what God is not. Enough to say that there are many confessedly Christian thinkers who feel that their faith can best be understood as a particular way of understanding one's place and possibilities in life, the man Jesus providing the key, the word and concept of God being allowed to disappear from the theological vocabulary.

3.4 Both these schools, the existentialists and the empiricists, have made constructive contributions to theology, not by what they say about God, but by criticizing traditional conceptions about what has been meant by the word 'God' in the past. In their own way, they draw attention to the classical distinction which theology has recognized for many centuries between (a) God as he affects and encounters us in our world (in classical terms, in creation and redemption) and (b) God as he is in himself. A description of the former, (a), would include reference to his operations, effects, his relations with the world; a description of the latter, (b), would include his absoluteness, his transcendence, his unique manner of existence (his 'aseity', as it was called).[2] They draw attention to the fact that when theology has been true to biblical thinking it has always maintained the mystery of God, his surpassing of all merely human concepts and attributes, so that there could be no question of giving an exhaustive description of God 'as he is in himself'. But it has maintained that on the basis of (a), that is, on the basis of what those who stand in the Judaeo-Christian tradition believe God has done in and to and for men in the world, supremely in Christ, and on the basis of our analysis of the way things are (philosophy), it is possible to speak of (b), indirectly and imperfectly, of course, but not misleadingly, by using the only language open to us, human language.

3.4.1 Unfortunately, past attempts to speak appropriately about (*b*) (God as he is in himself) were so successful and gained such universal recognition in the Western world that it was forgotten that they were only human attempts to describe a non-human reality. The analogical, makeshift character of these attempts was played down, and dropped out of consciousness, at least in the popular mind. What remained was the picture, accepted as a reality, of a transcendent being dwelling in a supernatural world apart. In theory, this reality was always acknowledged a mystery, but in practice it proved possible to say a great deal about him, or rather, it, since this particular approach tended to give the impression that what was being discussed was a thing. It had to be perfect, and therefore it was necessary to attribute to it freedom from all qualities which might be conceived of as weakness or imperfection. To be subject to chance and change, corruption and decay, was a sign of human weakness, therefore It must be immutable (incapable of being changed), impassible (incapable of being 'affected', and so of feeling or suffering), eternal, infinite, omnipotent, omniscient and so on. An unsympathetic observer might well see this as a sort of tailor's dummy approach: once the idea of God was arrived at, once the dummy was supplied, it seemed to be possible to deck it out in an endless variety of attributes as so many garments, by devising every manner of contrast with the finite human condition. A more sympathetic observer might draw attention to the fact that among the attributes with which the supernatural transcendent being was clothed was 'incomprehensibility', which might be a confession that all was not after all quite so straightforward as it appeared. He might also note that there were always those who were conscious of the radical mystery, even unknowability of God as he is in himself, who would gladly echo Pascal's dictum: 'Every religion which does not affirm that God is not hidden is not true.' A good case can also be made for saying that it is better boldly to take the risk of saying too much than too little on this unique and all-important subject. It must, however, be admitted that the picture which emerged was of a strange,

17

supernatural entity, conceived as a static thing with all kinds of qualities, standing beyond and above the things of this world, but still one thing among many.

3.4.2 This view of God is often now referred to as a 'metaphysical' understanding, because it presupposes a picture of reality consisting of two worlds, our world and a transcendent world beyond, in which this being, God, dwells. To many contemporary thinkers it is no longer tenable. The standard and apparently fatal criticisms are that it embodies a view of reality – a metaphysic, the two-world view – with which we no longer really work and that it makes God an object or thing, to be thought about and described in detachment like other physical things. It has also not escaped notice that this static, thing-like metaphysical being bears very little resemblance to the God of mystery yet vitality, dynamism and power of whom the Old and New Testaments speak.

3.4.3 One has every sympathy, therefore, with those who are so dissatisfied with this 'two-world' view of reality, with God as a supernatural, metaphysical entity in a world apart from our world. One can also readily concede that much of the talk about God in the past has presupposed the view that is now rejected, has presupposed, in other words, an alien metaphysic. But to deduce from that (with the existentialists) that it is now no longer possible to speak of God 'as he is in himself', but only as he encounters us and lets us understand ourselves anew, or (with the empiricists) that we may no longer speak of him meaningfully at all, is an expedient of despair warranted neither by the data on which it claims to be based nor by the demands of faith which, if it is to be liveable, must not be irrational. To replace a mythical giant in the sky with a giant-sized question mark can hardly be called an advance. The Gospel quite literally becomes 'news from nowhere'.

3.4.4 Part of the trouble is the general debasement of metaphysics which has been taking place this century, and which has profoundly affected both philosophy and theology. If the 'alien metaphysic' of the two-world view of reality were the only proper concern of the metaphysician, then when that view was discredited, the so-called science of metaphysics would automatically fall to the ground. But metaphysics is not the science of describing various alleged features of a mysterious other-world. The legitimate and necessary concern of the metaphysician is with 'how to take what happens here and now'. This he can do while keeping his feet planted quite firmly on the ground. His business is to spell out the view of reality presupposed in what people do and choose and hope. The most thoroughgoing materialist works with a particular metaphysic, a particular view of reality, every bit as much as the most other-worldly of mystics. If the one or the other refuses to recognize this and never allows it to come to consciousness or to become open to conscious inspection and criticism, he may get by, but the one thing he cannot claim is to be acting with consistency and reason. Nor is he in any position to challenge the fundamental presuppositions of those who do not share his attitude to life.

3.4.5 To the theologian, therefore, who puts a dogmatic ban on all talk of God 'as he is in himself' or indeed on talk of God at all, one must suggest that he is suffering from an unaccountable case of metaphysical jitters. If the Christian is not prepared to say – and this, for the moment, is putting it at its lowest – that he can give an adequate account of reality without bringing God into account, then he must be prepared to entertain the question, 'Who is God?' Moreover, he must finally admit that he is dealing with metaphysical questions. To answer that question, it is not, of course, necessary to write an entire treatise on metaphysics. But there can be no dodging of metaphysical questions. Protest against outworn metaphysical categories and an alien metaphysical system are justified only if they are replaced by something more constructive. In the end of the day, when truth and a comprehensive account of reality are at issue, there is not much to choose between metaphysical clouds and non-metaphysical sand.

4 So far we have been considering the apparent ban on

giving a straight answer to our question 'Who is God?' which certain theological insights would seem to demand. Our conclusion is that such insights may well serve as a warning and bid us proceed cautiously but need not, indeed should not, deter us. But it would be foolish to pretend that there are no other obvious obstacles in our path. One, in particular, deserves serious consideration. This is the ban imposed by those who believe that all talk about God must be neither true nor false, but meaningless, and therefore 'non-sense'. We ought to look at it with care, both in its negative and positive aspects.

4.1 Negatively, this ban is arrived at by showing that there is no valid proof of the existence of God: it is impossible to prove conclusively that God exists by any of the classical arguments – from the evidence of design in nature, from the alleged need of a First Cause to initiate and sustain causes and effects in the world, from existence of beings in the world implying the existence of a Supreme Being, from the moral sense in humanity implying a supreme moral lawgiver. All these arguments have been tried, and as proofs, have been found wanting. Further, what might be interpreted as religious experience cannot begin to add up to proof of the existence of God: for one thing, it may be purely subjective; for another, the bewildering variety of what is interpreted as religious experience, if it infers the existence of anything 'outside' the believer, is capable of inferring not one God but as many different gods as there are varieties of religious experience. Most decisive of all, it is argued, 'the religious hypothesis' of a sophisticated theism seems to entail no consequences which could serve to confirm or falsify it. 'So', we are told, 'if your theism is to have any factual ingredient you have got to find something for it to deny: "Just what would have to happen, or not happen, or to have happened, or not to have happened, to entitle us to say that – in your sense of the word – There is no God?" '.[3]

Now with much of this, the Christian believer in God must be sympathetic. We cannot prove (nor disprove) the existence of God, nor disprove his non-existence nor prove his non-existence. And we cannot state what would have to happen to entitle us to say, 'There is no God' – without, that is, appealing to anticipated situations in an after-life which again we cannot now prove or legitimately use as evidence. Indeed, we can go further and admit that there are times when most believers find themselves saying just that – 'There is no God' – though they may later know that at these times they have been speaking emotionally rather than rationally. But even granted that we can go a long way with the negative argument, we cannot and need not concede that it renders any idea of God meaningless. It all depends on the kind of God one has in mind. If God were merely a thing among things, an 'extra' to the world of sense and time, then the demand for proof or the specification of falsifying circumstances would be entirely justified. But if he is not that kind of being, if he is – but this is to anticipate – both transcendent (beyond everything in this world) and immanent (related to, in, behind or before everything that happens in this world), then the demand for the statement of falsifying circumstances becomes meaningless. And the God of Christian faith is precisely he of whom the believer may say, dangerously: 'Though he slay me, yet will I trust in him' (Job 13.15) or, more comprehensively: 'I am convinced that there is nothing in death or life, in the realm of spirits or superhuman powers, in the world as it is or the world as it shall be, in the forces of the universe, in heights or depths – nothing in all creation that can separate us from the love of God which is in Christ Jesus our Lord' (Rom. 8.38 f).

4.2 Positively, the ban on talk of God from this quarter arises from the acceptance as natural or even obvious of one particular metaphysic or set of presuppositions. Let us call this the atheist presumption. Technically, this presumption in question has been well expounded as follows: The presumption 'must be that all qualities observed in things are qualities belonging by natural right to those things themselves; and hence that whatever characteristics we think ourselves able to discern in the universe as a whole are the underivative characteristics of the universe itself'.[4]

This presumption, it is claimed, successfully dislodges any tendency to conclude from the fact that there is order in the universe and regularity in nature that there must be a super-natural Orderer or Regulator – a conclusion, incidentally, which few Christians would now want to draw. Further, behind this presumption lies the conviction which has been neatly described as 'This–is–all–there–is–ism, there–isn't–any–more–ism'. Reality consists in what is open for physical inspection, observable, testable, recordable here and now. This is enough to live by, to understand ourselves and our world by. There is no need to bring in God as a person or principle or hypothesis: this can only be a dangerous diversion, drawing men's eyes away from what they should be looking at and their hands from the plain task before them.

4.2.1　What are we to say of this presumption of 'this–is–all–there–is–ism'? Clearly it is not to be dismissed in cavalier fashion. It is the presumption which millions of men and women in the Western world think they are working with, and which many others, while denying it with their lips, are confessing with their lives. As a protest against the lack of attention and concern about what is going on in the world which preoccupation with a distant deity, unrelated to 'the changes and chances of this fleeting world', engenders, it is unquestionably salutary. In at least one way, too, it suggests a useful insight into the Christian view of God, to which we shall refer again later. Christians do not claim to see in the universe any more than the atheists see: the raw material is the same. Only they claim to see it in a different way. It was, after all, the apostle Paul who made the astonishing statement, 'For all that may be known of God by men lies plain before their eyes' (Rom. 1.19). What, then, is wrong with the presumption?

4.2.2　As an argument for atheism, the first thing to note is that it is a metaphysical presumption every bit as metaphysical as any other basic presumption, including the presumption of the existence of God. In itself, it cannot be proved or deduced from the things of the world. It can only be opted for and acted upon, consciously, or, more likely, unconsciously. It is built into one view of reality and not into other views of reality. It must take its place along with many other starters in what we may call the 'Reality Stakes', and be judged on its performance, no matter how heavily backed it may be or how low the starting price at this point of time. It has no weight advantage, and may be under a disadvantage, as we shall see, because of its jockey. It is certainly not in some non-metaphysical class by itself.

4.2.3 But secondly, and more importantly, it must be said that if this presumption excludes belief in God, it also excludes belief in man. For the presumption of 'this–is–all–there–is–ism' provides no more ground for believing that the welfare of man and woman, the human race, is of any special, not to say unique, importance, which is what the humanist so loyally maintains. It provides no basis for values, or standards, good or bad, no basis for morality. It is in line with this presumption to look at the evidence. One of its ablest exponents writes as follows: 'All our knowledge of things, of their natures and tendencies, has to be founded upon and checked against the ways those things in fact behave, under whatever conditions they can be available for our study'.[5] Granted. But let us substitute 'persons' for 'things' in that sentence, and ask quietly, how do persons in fact behave? The only answer we could give is: in every conceivable way – as brave and as cowards, as selfish and unselfish, as thinking and unthinking, as kind and as cruel, as dependent and as independent. For every Gandhi, we can find a Hitler, and for every hero a villain. Is this evidence from which one can draw any reliable conclusion as to what is good and what is bad, what is right and what is wrong? It is not only to the sadist that pleasure is pain: happiness for one man is misery for another; heaven for the saint is hell for the sinner.

Yet people also act, and cannot live without acting, on the basis that some things are more in tune with reality than others, that some actions are better than others, right and wrong, that some aims are more worthwhile than others. Christians, let it be said, have no corner in moral values or

23

human concern. Many atheists today are taking the lead in the fight to uphold the dignity of man, to promote human values, to care for their fellows, particularly the under-privileged and oppressed. Far from denying this, those who do not share the atheist presupposition should welcome the fact, and see it as a just rebuke to their own vacillations. But it still holds that the humanist convictions simply do not follow from the initial presumption, any more than rationalism, or radicalism, or nihilism. What makes a man care passionately for his fellows is not the simple knowledge that 'this–is–all–there–is'. It is his understanding of what ultimately matters, of his perspective on 'all–that–there–is'. If his presumption makes theism irrational, atheist humanism must suffer from the same defect.

The point is not that to know right from wrong, good from bad, you have to believe in God. Morality does not require a God to endorse and to enforce moral claims with some-thing like supernatural authority. But it does require a decision as to what ultimately matters, it demands a view of reality. And this view of reality must be more than an exhaustive catalogue of everything we can see, touch, examine and measure: it must be some kind of shape or whole in which all that is held together.

5 Thus far, we have been trying to indicate some of the hurdles that have to be overcome by anyone who is trying to say what he is doing when he is using the word 'God'. We have rejected the procedure of proving *that* a being called God exists, of showing *what* he must be like and then acknowledging *who* he is. We have looked at and taken to heart the warnings of those theologians who bid us restrict our talk of God to his effects on us, on how we are to understand ourselves, keeping silence on the question of God 'as he is in himself'. Finally, we looked briefly at the claims made by those thinkers who believe that the evidence is not such as to dislodge the presumption of 'this–is–all–there–is', who insist that because believers cannot suggest any circumstances which would lead them to conclude, 'There is no God', talk of God is neither true nor false but non-sense. We have not been satisfied that any of these objections is compelling enough to force us to abandon the project of trying to answer the question, 'Who is God?' On the contrary, we have suggested that whether they like it or not, everyone in fact and in practice, consciously or unconsciously, works and acts on the basis of some view of reality, a view which cannot be proved and which is not a mere deduction from the so-called brute facts of life. But now, trying to bear in mind the insights which the objections just considered afford, we must try to be more positive.

6   The Christian conviction is that it is impossible to give shape to reality, including all the brute facts of life and including ourselves, without using the word 'God'. If the Christian were asked, 'What ultimately matters?', or, 'What is real?', and tried to answer without using the word God, he would not be speaking with superior wisdom or humanity or integrity: he would simply be lying.[6] He could not give an account of reality on the presumption of 'this–is–all–there–is', at least in the ordinary sense, because for him 'all–there–is' must include experience, intuitions, perceptions, convictions which he cannot put to the test or play about with for the purpose of proof. The only way he can put them to the test is by acting on them: not to act on them is to deny them. The positive starting point for our enquiry as to who God is must therefore be to say that it is an attempt to articulate the Christian view of what ultimately matters. Before, however, we can proceed, certain preliminary points must be made to clear the ground and avoid misunderstandings which could vitiate the whole exercise.

6.1   When the Christian says that God is what ultimately matters for him, he is *not* inviting the conclusion that nothing that is not God matters. We shall have to return to this when we consider (see Chapter 4) how God is related to our world and our lives of sense and time, but the point is worth making now because it is so often just assumed by non-Christians that the very idea of God carries with it inescapable world-denying associations. It is, of course, true that at times the Christian Church has behaved and taught

25

in such a way as to give rise to this assumption, as if what was real was not only not of this world but barely related to this world, so that escape from this world was the aim of life. But a comprehensive survey of the history of Christian doctrine would reveal that this assumption was never really justified.

Each age discovers new implications of the Christian view of reality, and one of the most exciting re-discoveries which Christians have made over the last hundred years is that because God became man in Jesus Christ, thereby assuming the conditions of this world and life, the correct conclusion to draw is not God's essential indifference to the world of sense and time but, on the contrary, his supreme concern for it. There is, then, no built-in other-worldliness in the Christian's view of reality.

6.2　Here, too, it must be admitted that there is no such thing as neutral knowledge of God. Put thus baldly, this may appear both disappointing and extreme, giving the game away before it has begun. And certainly, it does imply that there is no way of describing God in such a way as the open, fair-minded, uncommitted observer simply must accept as true if he is determined to be logical. But it equally does not imply that therefore there is no God. All it does imply is that the person talking about God is already in some way committed to a view of reality in which he and God are involved. His language about God is self-involving, it takes in his convictions not about some one thing or being, but about everything that is, including himself. Thus his knowledge of God cannot be abstracted from his knowledge of what ultimately matters about other people, other things, and himself.

6.2.1　There is rather a depressing maxim which has recently enjoyed a certain vogue in theology: 'Faith cannot argue with unbelief.' This seems fairly effectively to close the door to any discussion between believers and agnostics and atheists and is therefore an aggressive exaggeration of the situation. 'Faith' can certainly try to articulate its view of what ultimately matters, and invite 'unbelief' to point out any inconsistencies and contradictions in it. 'Unbelief', too, can articulate its view of what ultimately matters, and invite constructive criticisms of it. In such exercises nothing but good can come. But there is truth in the maxim if it is taken only to mean that faith cannot offer convincing proof by means of argument. All it can do is to hold before unbelief the new possibility of a different way of understanding reality.

6.2.2 It is perhaps worth noting that God is not the only subject with regard to which we must say that no neutral knowledge is possible. Consider a very simple illustration. Mr X and Mr Y have been friends since schooldays. In their youth they used to go on holidays together; Mr Y was Mr X's best man, and as it happens, Mr X and Mr Y, and in due course their children, get on famously and see a great deal of each other. This friendship continues: they take it as a matter of course that they should discuss their problems, business and personal, and if there is anyone Mr X can trust outside the family it is Mr Y. One day – they are both by now in their sixties – a newcomer to the town, Mr Z, approaches Mr Y, tells him he is interested in Mr X's firm but that something fishy is going on and that he has a hunch that Mr X is at the bottom of it. 'Nonsense!', explodes Mr Y. 'It couldn't be X, dammit, I know him.' Of course, Mr Y could have been deceived, or just wrong. Mr Z might be able to unearth certain facts which a court of law might accept as substantiating his suspicions, though, in the event, Mr Y would probably insist that there must have been extenuating factors which would relieve Mr X of moral guilt in his eyes. But there is a sense in which Mr Y, must be right. When we are talking about a whole person, and not just about the colour of his hair, the state of his arteries or his ability to do this or that, there can be no final objective evidence. There is, of course, evidence, the cumulative evidence of Mr Y's total experience of Mr X, and his acted-on trust of Mr X, but this must always be evidence of a kind which can only speak to Mr Y. This means that statements of the 'it–couldn't-be–X, dammit–I–know–him' variety are indeed meaningful, but they also point to the fact that when a whole person is concerned, neutral knowledge, not directly involving the attitude of the knower, is out of the question. The things we want to say about God have much in common with statements of that kind.

7 This point leads us on naturally to ask what sort of evidence is to count for our statements about God. Even if neutral knowledge is impossible, we have seen that 'it couldn't be X, dammit I know him' was a statement supported by evidence of a special kind. But on what kind of evidence do we base our knowledge of God? What, in other words, are the data on the basis of which theological statements are to be judged true or false?

7.1 As we have indicated, a Christian is one who accepts as his own a particular understanding of what matters most, of ultimate reality, and this includes his own place and possibilities within and *vis-à-vis* this reality. But it is not just his private view. It is his own, but there is nothing individualistic about it. He did not dream it up or think it up or reason it out or stumble upon it. He may have received it in any one or combination of a variety of ways: he may have grown up in it and always taken it for granted, or he may only have arrived at it gradually after a long and painful course of doubting, suspicion and questioning, so that there could be no question of his dating his acceptance; by contrast, it may have come to consciousness after some cataclysmic experience, turning his emotions inside out. But the variety of ways in which this understanding is arrived at, however multifarious, should not be allowed to obscure one important fact. This particular understanding of reality can only originate in one particular place, and that place is a particular historical community of men and women and children, namely the Church. It is received as response to the Church's proclamation. This does not mean that only in *a* church or in response to some particular sermon or series of services is this understanding mediated: proclamation may take the form of action or consistent attitudes as well as preaching. But it does mean that it is mediated only through people and through people in community, the particular community who, however imperfectly, lives by this particular understanding. We are, of course, here referring to the community whose unifying feature is acceptance of Jesus as the Christ, or as of decisive and unique significance in understanding and responding to reality. The first thing to be said of the data for Christian knowledge of God is that it is the data accepted as authoritative in this community on the basis of its collective experience.

7.2 It is tempting to simplify and put this another way. It is tempting to say that Christians are those who accept Jesus as the key to reality. This would be true, but it would not be the whole truth. For one thing, put like that it could imply that once we have used the key to open the door to reality we could throw it away and forget about it. For Christians such is not the case: Jesus is more than the occasion of coming to terms with reality, his significance is not only decisive but it is permanent and irreplaceable. For another thing, it would imply that it is a comparatively simple matter to know what there is to know about Jesus, which again is not the case. The situation is not that we have on the one hand the 'historical facts' about the man Jesus and on the other the claims made by his disciples for Jesus, or the interpretation of the Church. We simply have no record or knowledge of Jesus apart from the claims made by his disciples: all we know of him is told on the presupposition of the claims made on his behalf, so that it is impossible to dissect 'fact' from interpretation. If the language of fact and interpretation is going to be used at all, it can only be that fact and interpretation together form the data for our knowledge of who Jesus is.

7.2.1 Another way of expressing this is to look for a moment at the way the Gospel comes to us. It comes to us through the New Testament, which presents the history of Jesus as the good news or gospel of God, or as we might say, the truth about reality. It comes to us in the form of a story, but a story from which the last chapter is missing. This last chapter is, however, provided – but by the person who hears the story. It is he who writes the last chapter when he says with his lips and his life: this is the truth, or this is a pack of lies. The Church is the community of those who have in one way or another given the former answer and in their lives have confirmed for themselves that, to put it crudely, it is not only true but works.

7.2.2 This story, however, is no mere fairy tale, or construction of the poetic imagination. It concerns the historical man Jesus. All we know of him, we know from the collection of books known as the New Testament, and therefore the New Testament constitutes a large part of our data for our acceptance of what matters most. But the New Testament cannot begin to make sense without the Old Testament. The earliest Christians had no New Testament; all they had was the Old Testament interpreted by Jesus, and verbal accounts of this interpretation of reality. Indeed, one might go the length of saying that the New Testament can only be understood when it is seen as an authoritative commentary on the Old. Jesus himself was a Jew, living in a Jewish community. He had no 'hot line to God': all he knew of reality was gathered from the scriptures of the Old Testament and the worship of his Jewish contemporaries. There can therefore be no question of getting to grips with, far less responding to his view of reality, unless we are going to include the Old Testament with the New in our data.

7.3 It would, however, be naïve to say that the Christian's data for his understanding of reality is simply the Bible, the Testaments Old and New. The Bible is a difficult book and one which can be used, and alas frequently is, to provide supporting texts for all sorts of notions which have essentially nothing to do with Christian knowledge. By digging around for isolated texts the racist, the fanatic, the sadist, the flat-earther, the nihilist, the hermit can all come up with some comfort. Therefore we must refer back to our first point – that the Christian view of reality is a shared, community view – and say that reality for the Christian is reality both testified to in the Bible and experienced and verified in the historical experience of the Christian community. This means that the past and present experience of the Church forms part of the data.

7.3.1 The experience of community in the past is never of merely academic interest: it forms part of the data of our knowledge of reality now. But the experience of the community in the past must be integrated with its experience in the present and, indeed, judged in the light of the present. If past experience – and in this we would have to include past formulations of doctrine – has the effect of dominating or denying present experience, then it would be folly to speak of either freedom, or of openness to reality now. The individual who lives in the past is a tragic spectacle; so is the community. Therefore, included in our data of reality must be the present experience of the Christian community. For us, this means this will be the experience of twentieth-century men and women, with the ways of thinking and talking and doing of other twentieth-century men and women. When it is our turn to talk about and respond to reality, it will be and will have to be in twentieth-century language and twentieth-century ways. Without ceasing to be ourselves, we could do no other. We are aware that experience is not an infallible guide; but to attempt to deny present experience is to turn one's back on truth and escape into illusion.

7.3.2 In speaking of the experience of the Christian community as providing the data for our knowledge of God, we have tried to avoid giving the impression that Christian faith is primarily an individualistic affair. But now it must be said that community experience is shared experience, and this implies that individuals do in fact share in such experience. Community experience can act as a useful support and provide a reliable check on and standard for an individual's interpretation of his own experience, but it can never render it irrelevant. Unless an individual can give the community experience his personal backing as his very own, unless he can say for himself, 'I know whom I have believed', then his identification with the community and his acceptance of its beliefs will be purely formal. A second-hand faith is the soil of 'double-think', logically suspicious and psychologically dangerous. So it must be insisted that the individual's response to reality, his actions and reactions, his thoughts, fears, hopes and feelings – in short his experience in the broadest sense – must be included in the data.

8 The data, then, for Christian statements about God can be summed up as the total experience of that community which accepts the man Jesus as being decisive, and it includes the Bible, the experience of the community (including the individual in the community) in the past and the experience (including the way people think) of the present. In putting it this way, we are trying to provide the means whereby what we say about God may be judged true or false. Theology is not an exact science, but neither is it, as many of its critics seem to suppose, a tedious compendium of wishful thoughts. Theological statements can be false as well as true (e.g. two false statements are: 'God hates sinners'; 'In the eyes of God, all men are not of equal value'), and they are known to be true or false by being justified or not justified (or, indeed, verified) by the data. Earlier, we said there was no neutral knowledge of God. But this did not mean that there is no real knowledge of God, only subjective feelings. It means that though no one can be forced to accept the data, for those who do accept it, knowledge of God is knowledge in the fullest and truest sense.

In presenting the data as we have done, we are in effect denying that there is anything like a holy language available to Christians for speech about God. In the English-speaking world, adherence to the Authorized Version of the Bible has sometimes given this impression. But the growing use of modern translations is rapidly dispelling this notion, which should have been recognized as false all along. Sometimes, Christians are too concerned about communicating their view of reality to others before they have really worked it out for themselves. They worry about the problem of communication and the apparent difficulty of putting what they want to say into words which others understand. The prior question, however, is putting it into words which they themselves understand: mere repetition of phrases and formulae in an alien language, from a bygone age, is not worth communicating anyway. Of course, as St Paul reminds us, even speaking with the tongues of men is of no help without love, but to speak with the tongues of angels is for us an impossibility.

9 In this introduction, an attempt has been made to pave the way for answering the question, 'Who is God?' After trying to show why it is impossible to proceed on the basis of proving the existence of God and then 'analysing' him, we considered some of the objections of those – Christians and non-Christians – who fear that any attempt to answer this question must be doomed to failure. As against them, we maintained that the onus is on the Christian, despite all the pitfalls, to give some answer to our question. We then indicated that Christians use the word 'God' to indicate what is of ultimate importance, what is really real for them. Because this involves everything that is and demands a total response, there can be no neutral, uncommitted, uninvolved knowledge of God: he is not 'proveable', but equally he is not meaningless; on the contrary, he gives meaning to those committed to him. After that we looked at the data for Christian knowledge of God, the standard by which the truth or adequacy of what we say is to be judged. We now conclude this introduction with a reminder of danger, or at least potential trouble ahead.

9.1 In offering an answer to our question, we are not claiming to know all there is to know about God. What ultimately matters to Christians is something which is to be encountered in their experience of life and so can be thought about and talked about. But it vastly transcends their experience and thinking. More strongly, it discloses itself as a mystery, and does not cease to be a mystery after the disclosure. Is not this, after all, a confession of total agnosticism? The Christian answers confidently in the negative, because the mystery which discloses itself does so as a mystery which can be trusted, acted upon and worshipped and which therefore can be spoken of. The Christian recognizes that this mystery is more than human, and that as there is no non-human or holy language in which to describe it, his descriptions must be inadequate. But they need not be inappropriate, because this mystery discloses itself supremely in a human life lived, in Jesus of Nazareth, the man who finally justifies human speech about God.

9.2 Theology in the past has not hesitated to speak of the 'unknowability' or 'incomprehensibility' of God. To modern ears this may sound strange and indeed place a question-mark against the whole theological enterprise. All it really means, however, is that God cannot be 'mastered' by human minds, cannot be completely 'accounted for', conceptualized and brought to expression in human categories. In the words of the once popular expression, he is to be addressed, not expressed. But our statements about him will be true, even though these are in human language and concepts, if they do justice to the data; in a sense, they can and must be checked with the data, and will therefore not be merely arbitrary. Our theological statements will not be valid for all time, since language and thought forms are constantly changing and what a word means now may well be something quite different from what it meant even one hundred years ago or from what it may mean one hundred years hence. But it will be valid for our time to the extent that on the basis of its data it uses appropriate images or models, or modes of speech which speak to and in our time. Yet though valid, it will never be exhaustive and complete, because the reality it talks about comprises depths unfathomable and riches unsearchable. It can, then, only properly be engaged in a spirit of humility and openness on all sides to that which is yet to come.

NOTES

1. C. A. van Peursen, 'Man and Reality: The History of Human Thought', *Student World* 56 (1963), pp. 13–21; also in John Bowden and James Richmond (eds.), *A Reader in Contemporary Theology* (London: SCM Press; Philadelphia: Westminster Press, 1967), pp. 115–26; quoted in J. A. T. Robinson, *Exploration into God* (London: SCM Press; Stanford University Press, 1967), p. 40.

2. The word comes from the Latin *a se*, 'from himself'. 'Whatever he has, he has from himself.'

3. For this paragraph see A. Flew, *God and Philosophy* (London: Hutchinson, 1966), pp. 170 f.

4. See A. Flew, *op. cit.*, p. 69.

5. A. Flew, *op. cit.*, p. 72.

6. Even 'Death of God' theologians, if they claim to be expounding Christian insights, do not attempt to answer these questions without recourse to something which, on examination, transcends what can be seen, touched, examined, etc., e.g. 'the contagious freedom of Jesus', 'the contemporary form of Christ in the world', 'the *gift* of authentic existence'.

2 God as 'Who'

1 In the first chapter, we tried to deal with some of the preliminary questions inevitably facing anyone seeking an intelligible answer to the question 'Who is God?' We indicated that when we use the word 'God' we are not talking about some thing or entity among other things or entities, but are trying to articulate 'what matters most'. A Christian speaking of God does not and cannot pretend for the purposes of argument that he is not a Christian or is capable of speaking from some neutral standpoint. So for him the basis of knowledge of God is the whole of reality (including human reason) experienced within that community which accepts Jesus as being decisive for both understanding and living. There being no holy, sacrosanct language available to us in which we might speak of God, or which might by its very use guarantee the correctness of our statements about God, we must make do with what we have, our everyday language, acknowledging that we have to do with a mystery but yet able, by the use of models which do justice to the facts, to speak truly and with enough confidence to act on. In this chapter, we proceed to speak more concretely, and investigate how and why God is to be thought of as 'who' rather than 'what'. In other words, we shall look at the use of the personal model for speech concerning God. In the process, we shall try to show why this is the first rather than the last aspect of the matter we should look at, and what we are doing when we think of God in personal terms. But it would be as well at the moment to refer briefly to two potential drawbacks.

2.1 If we say that the first thing to be said about God is that he is to be thought of in personal terms, are we not doing the one thing that so many contemporary theologians warn us against? Are we not committing ourselves irrevocably to the 'giant-in-the-sky' approach which has been found so inadequate, misleading or just plain wrong? Is this not an impossible approach for those who know that God is not shut off from our world and our life, leading a lonely existence in splendid isolation in some other world above the clouds or beyond clear blue skies? The reader will have to judge this for himself, but for the moment, let us simply reply to the charge: 'Not necessarily'. To adhere to the personal model, to say that God is to be spoken of in personal terms is not necessarily to say that he is 'a person'. If to say that God is personal necessarily meant (as undoubtedly some people naturally assume it means) that God is a person in this sense: I am a person, you are a person, Smith is a person, and then there's this person called 'God' – we would be in trouble, and would have to consider giving up talk of God as being primarily personal. There would not be much to choose between 'a thing among things' and 'a person among persons', and we have already rejected the former. But it does not follow that to speak of God in personal terms is to make him such a *person*. It only follows that we are ascribing personality (in a number of senses to be investigated) to him, and this is not the same thing. It might be added for the benefit of the suspicious that this is no exclusive theological dodge. Lawyers have no hesitation in ascribing personality (corporate personality) to certain institutions – to companies, to councils or even the State. John Galsworthy in 'The Forsyte Saga' was able to ascribe it to a family, and Hitler to one race. In principle, at least, there is no difficulty.

2.2 The second potential drawback is that to speak of God primarily in personal terms is to run the risk of walking right into the 'projection trap'. This particular trap is that laid, in their different ways, by the philosopher Feuerbach and the psychologist Freud, who maintained that God is an invention of the human race. Mankind, so the argument goes, aware of its basic insecurity, the brevity of life, its

37

weakness and frailties, unconsciously invents religion to satisfy, in the hereafter, if not here, all its basic needs and desires. It 'projects' into an 'other world', immune from the changes and chances of this world, all the qualities it envies but does not fully possess, depositing them in an alleged infinite, eternal, all-powerful super-human being called 'God', who then guarantees for mankind everything it hopes for but does not yet have. This account of religion, with its explaining-away of God as the product of wishful thinking, is so widely accepted as to be almost part of the conventional wisdom of the intelligentsia of the Western world. Is it not fatal to our contention that the first thing we want to say of God is that he is to be thought of in personal terms?

This is not the place to look in detail at the arguments of Feuerbach and Freud, though both still have much to teach the theologian. Two comments are, however, relevant. First, to give an account of the origin of a belief is to say nothing as to its truth or falsehood. Second, the Freudian-Feuerbachian critique of religion, if true, is applicable not just to the Christian or any other religion, but to any view of what ultimately matters, to any view of reality, including Feuerbach's and Freud's. An old illustration from a slightly different context may help to clarify both points. Archbishop William Temple is said on one occasion to have been addressing a high-powered, free-thinking student audience. One student could not restrain himself and blurted out: 'You only believe what you believe because of your early upbringing.' To which the Archbishop replied: 'And you only believe that I only believe what I believe because of my early upbringing because of your early upbringing.' Boldness of argument is of itself no defence against circularity. We dare not forget Feuerbach and Freud. But we shall try to use their arguments constructively, not to reduce us to silence but to check our assumptions and the things we take for granted against our data, letting them remind us of the danger of substituting desires for data.

3 Why, then, do we want to begin by speaking of God in personal terms, as 'Who?' The short and only valid

answer is that this is demanded by our data. If this statement is to be justified, it will have to be related to the biblical evidence, to the continuous testimony of the Church and to the experience of the modern Christian.

3.1 It would be both foolish and misleading to pretend that in their thought of God any of the biblical writers consciously used anything which might correspond to our modern notion of personality. Nor, if we were so minded, could we point to any text in the Bible which says unequivocally 'God is personal' – as we can when we are talking about God as love (1 John 4.8). Yet it would be equally foolish to deny that in the Old and New Testaments, God is spoken of primarily in personal terms. To be sure, in the Old Testament there is no shortage of apparently impersonal metaphors used of God, words like 'fortress', 'rock', 'high tower', 'sun and shield' – the list could be indefinitely extended. But when these impersonal metaphors are used, their purpose is obviously functional, and the function they are intended to indicate is not incompatible with a personal function: the significance of the 'fortress' or the 'high tower' is not what they are made of but what they do; they 'protect': 'rock' can be 'relied on' and so forth.

3.1.1 However that may be, the Israelites were unquestionably predisposed to think of God in personal terms. Indeed, for all their consciousness of the majesty and mystery of God, their ways of referring to him can be riotously anthropomorphic; human, that is, writ large. He can laugh and be angry, he can see (and deliberately look the other way), he can hear (and turn a deaf ear). All kinds of human emotions and activities can be ascribed to him.

Aside from this wealth of anthropomorphic reference, God in the Old Testament is supremely to be thought of as the One who acts, who created the heavens and the earth, and man 'in his own image and likeness', who takes the initiative in covenant and commitment to save his elect nation, who punishes them for their disobedience, who communes with his chosen leaders, who declares his promises and can be relied on to keep them. As has been said, no notion of personality as we understand it is consciously worked out or articulated. But the pointers towards such a notion are too abundant in the Old Testament to deny.

3.1.2 In the New Testament, these pointers stand out even more clearly; one might say, unequivocally. To borrow St Mark's phrase, the New Testament is 'the good news of Jesus Christ the Son of God' (Mark 1.1), and for our present purpose, this immediately introduces two new factors: first, the terms in which Jesus himself referred to God and, second, the terms in which Jesus is proclaimed as Lord.

3.1.2.1 The God of whom Jesus spoke and taught was, of course, none other than the God of whom the Old Testament prophets had spoken and the source of his knowledge of God was none other than the scriptures of the Old Testament and the worship of the synagogue. It is not, then, surprising that scholars analysing, for example, the Sermon on the Mount have been able to show that Jesus was not teaching 'out of the blue', but was drawing on and developing Old Testament insights. But his originality was his emphasis, and his emphasis was on God as Father. God was his Father, whose will he had been sent to do. He taught his disciples to pray to God as 'our Father', to rely on him as on One who had a universal care and concern for creation and his creatures, a care and concern which could best be understood as the relation of a father to his children. Righteousness, justice, the consequences of selfishness and sin are not played down, but a new feature – again not absent from the Old Testament – now comes to prominence. God is the One who forgives, who accepts even the outcast and lawbreaker. Real life, Jesus taught his disciples, consisted in the closest possible personal communion with God, not as mystical isolation but with worship and trust issuing in attitudes towards other people after the manner of his own compassion and concern, on the basis of the fatherly compassion and concern of God. Once men start thinking of God as Father in this way, it is unlikely that they can ever think of him otherwise than in personal terms.

40

3.1.2.2 When we turn to the second aspect of New Testament teaching, what is otherwise unlikely is now seen to be impossible. For Jesus is remembered in the New Testament not solely for the quality of his teaching or for the example of his life. The earliest Christian confession, 'Jesus is Lord', is a shorthand summary of the many different titles by which the Early Church proclaimed its Head. We need recall only a few of these titles – the Anointed One, the Messiah, the Christ; Son of God, Word of God made flesh, Lamb of God, God's Elect; the bearer of the Spirit, the Light of the World; Reconciler, Redeemer, Saviour. Yet all these exalted titles were applied not to some demi-god or phantom apparition or legendary hero, but to a flesh and blood man, living a real human life, dying a real human death at a specific point of time and in a specific social setting. One of the main functions of theology from that time on has been to try to find words for the relationship between God the Father and this man Jesus, to try to say who Jesus is. As the meaning of language changes, the successful formulae of one age have to give way to the reformulations of another. But however strange some of the formulations may now appear, one thing is indisputable: for the earliest Christians who wrote the New Testament, as for the most modern, God and Jesus are so closely related that there could never be any question of thinking of one in isolation from the other. To speak of God is to speak implicitly of Jesus, to speak of Jesus is to speak implicitly of God. Further, what is implicit becomes explicit when Jesus is made the subject of worship and prayer. Generation after generation of Christians have followed the example of the New Testament Church in this without any sense of blasphemy. Similarly, they have acknowledged that in matters of service and obedience and acceptance of forgiveness, the name of Jesus is synonymous with God.

3.2 In brief, then, if the biblical evidence is in any sense decisive for our understanding of God – and for Christians it is – then it is overwhelmingly in favour of understanding God as personal. This remains true, even when we admit, as

41

we must, that the Bible does not work with any concept (ancient or modern) of personality. Our next task is to see how this biblical insight has been received and worked out in the Church.

3.2.1 Here we must introduce a distinction, the importance of which increases proportionately to the extent to which it is ignored. This is the distinction between 'personality in God' and 'personality of God'. In these two phrases, the same word 'personality' appears, but it is used in very different senses, which require clarification. This is not the place to embark on a history of Christian thought in this regard, but we shall see that the latter way of thinking – 'personality of God' – is of much more recent origin than the former – 'personality in God' – which we therefore consider first.

3.2.1.1 Reference has already been made to the attempts of the Early Church to put into words the relationship that existed between God and Jesus. Now we must investigate this a little more closely, for it was in this connection that the idea of personality in God was developed. Jesus was a Jew in a Jewish community, and his first disciples were Jews. Without question, they shared the uncompromising, not to say fierce monotheism of Israelite religion. The Jews were familiar with the idea of a Messiah, a man specially chosen by God to bring triumph, glory and prosperity to his nation. But this Messiah was not to be equated with God himself: at most he was to be thought of as God's emissary or nominee. Now the earliest Christians certainly proclaimed Jesus as the Messiah. But as they tried to remain faithful to their convictions and experience – their view of reality – doing justice to the human Jesus whom they had known and also to their conviction that the death of this man was not the end of the story, but rather the beginning, they found that they could not do less than ascribe to Jesus the honour and dignity that had hitherto been reserved exclusively for God (e.g. Col. 2.3, 9). It was not that they ceased to be monotheists, as if Jesus were a second God alongside the Creator God of the Old Testament. Rather they found that if they were to do justice to all the evidence – their belief in God, their knowledge of the man Jesus, the conviction of his constant presence with them – they had to think of the one God in a new way – as Father, Son and Holy Spirit. Of course, the first-generation Christians did not calmly sit down and think out a complete doctrine of the Trinity. But there are enough references in the New Testament and other early Christian writings to enable us to say that in their speech, thought and above all their worship, they spontaneously began to use a concept of God which later theologians could analyse in Trinitarian terms (e.g. Matt. 28.19; John 14; Acts 2.33; II Cor. 13.14).

3.2.1.2 What has all this to do with 'personality in God'? Simply this: in the ensuing centuries, as Christians tried to find concepts to express adequately the God of Christian salvation and communicate their understanding of one God who could at one and the same time be Father, Son and Holy Spirit, they drew on contemporary philosophical resources and appropriated the technical Greek logical term 'hypostasis' (translated in Latin 'persona' and in English 'person') to denote the divine mode of existence of the one God as Father or as Son or as Holy Spirit. It is easy for us to feel impatient and possibly exasperated at the endless argument that went on among the early Fathers of the Church over the details of Trinitarian theology, though a little imagination should enable us to see that they were not arguing over words so much as over the nature of reality for Christians. However that may be, agreement was finally reached which was adequate to all the evidence, and this was on the basis of One God in three persons, Father, Son, and Holy Spirit.

3.2.1.3 It would require a long digression at this point to plot the exact meaning of 'hypostasis' or 'person' in post-Aristotelian philosophy, which was its proper milieu. Broadly speaking, it might be characterized as subject, or substratum, the concrete individual in whom some general form or nature is particularized, with the double marks of intelligible character and concrete independence. The classical definition was given by Boethius in the sixth century: *'Person is an individual subsistence of a rational nature.'* Even a brief description like this is sufficient to indicate that here is a term belonging to a way of thinking utterly remote from our own practices or experience. We simply do not think in terms of 'forms' or 'natures' or 'substances' or 'subsistences' any more, and we need not pretend to. But it has been necessary to give some account of the use of the word 'person' with reference to the triune God in order to show how remote this original application of 'person' to God is from anything we mean by 'person' today. In its Trinitarian use, person is a logical term or model which has its home in a specific metaphysical system, which belongs to our past but not our present history. Yet this was the original sense in which personality was ascribed to God, as three persons *in* the one Godhead. We shall reserve for later consideration whether this sense of personality can in any way be blended or put to service in harmony with our more familiar sense of personality. But now we must examine what is meant by saying that God is personal in such a way as enables us to speak of personality *of* God.

3.2.2 We are, of course, still speaking of the Church's articulation of biblical insights when we speak of personality of God. But now we are speaking of personality in the modern sense of what makes a person a person, a sense which owes much to the psychological approach which has become almost natural for us and very little to the approach of our forefathers, who thought in terms of definition. This is another way of saying that in the sense under discussion we are using 'personality' as a psychological model to help us speak accurately of God, having largely abandoned (at least in our actual thinking) the older logical model of personality. How this shift in thinking or change of model came about is a complex and intriguing question. Among the factors which brought it about could certainly be included reaction against the impersonal absolutes of idealist philosophy of the eighteenth and nineteenth centuries; the invasion of psychology into all human enterprises (and theology no less than philosophy is a human enterprise); growing insight into our way of knowing other selves; the re-discovery by liberal theologians that Jesus was primarily to be thought of not as a strange construct of two 'natures', one human, one divine, but first and foremost as a real flesh-and-blood man; and the later overwhelming emphasis on Christology, the person of Christ, as normative for all our knowledge of God. No doubt other factors, too, were relevant, but the point to be made is that the modern insistence on personality (in the psychological sense as opposed to its meaning in classical logic) as being appropriately ascribed to God is a development of the last hundred years or so. Its comparative modernity is no drawback, for it allows us to hold together a number of things we want to say about God while at the same time helping to explain and give coherence to the evidence with which we have to work.

More important, however, than the history of the rise of this concept of personality and its application to God is the question of what it is used to convey. We do not attempt a definition of personality – simply because a person ceases to be a person when he is defined. All we can do is to describe some of the characteristics which make it appropriate to call God personal in this modern sense.

3.2.2.1 The first to be mentioned is uniqueness or singularity. Tom, Dick and Harry may have many things in common, there may not be much to choose between them for most practical purposes, but we can only say that Tom is a person if, when the chips are down, we recognize that Tom is Tom and not Dick or Harry. This rather obvious comment can be amplified by drawing into service a word well tried in the older theology. 'Uniqueness' here is being used in the sense of 'incommunicability'. Tom may communicate with other people, at his best he can give himself to others, but he cannot, while he lives, cease to be Tom. There is something about him which he cannot part with. Because he is a person, he cannot pass over into a different kind of thing. This is not to say that he is prevented in some way from acting in an impersonal or unworthy way. Nor does it mean that he has some guarantee against being treated by other people not as a person but as a thing. But it does mean that if he loses his uniqueness, that aspect of him which is incommunicable, he ceases to be Tom.

This element of uniqueness which we claim to be a feature of personality has traditionally been recognized, under the name of incommunicability, as applicable to God. It is true that Christian orthodoxy thought of incommunicability in static terms, as one of many attributes of God, without associating it in any way with personality. Nevertheless, even though we depart from the language of static attributes, this word still denotes certain important things we can say of God. For instance, God creates – the universe, you, me, Mao Tse Tung – without losing anything of himself or becoming something different. This is why Christian doctrine has always insisted that creation is not to be equated in any way with emanation. God can bring into being something other than himself without ceasing to be himself. Or again, when Christians have been pondering the miracle of the Incarnation, of the Word made flesh, they have always insisted that in becoming man in Jesus Christ, God has not made himself a third kind of being, something or someone half-man, half-God. Even if now our emphasis must be on Jesus as wholly man, yet it remains true that in him, God remains God. Or yet again, when Christians have wanted to speak of God's work in the world and have spoken of the Holy Spirit working in and through men and women, they have always resisted the idea that he becomes a part of human beings, a little bit of him in us. He remains himself. His uniqueness does not prejudice his action, his being in relation with what is 'outside' him. But equally, his identity, his 'self' is preserved. This is one aspect of the matter which justifies our seeing here an indicator of personality.

3.2.2.2 The second such indicator of personality to be mentioned is self-consciousness, or rather consciousness of self and of others. If we ask what is it that distinguishes a person from a machine or a collection of atoms or a bundle of instincts, then part of the answer we are entitled to give is that it is a characteristic of a person that he knows that he exists, he is aware of himself as existing even though at moments he may doubt the existence of anything else. When we speak of the divine self-consciousness, we are trying to bring to expression the acknowledgment that together with any encounter with God comes the conviction of being in the presence of a personal reality who exists for himself, before we ever existed for him. He exists in and for himself even before he exists for us, indeed his existence in and for himself, or his 'aseity' (see p. 16 above), as an older theology would put it, is the presupposition of his real existence for us. In more modern terms, his reality does not depend on the reality of creation; that which encounters us from beyond is not dissolved in the actual encounter. While all our knowledge of him is based on our relation to him, we cannot satisfactorily account for this relation unless we take the further step of acknowledging that he is real, exists, apart from that relation.

The expression 'self-consciousness' was qualified to cover consciousness of self *and of others*. These last three words are important, for another characteristic of personality is the ability to communicate with, to be concerned for, and even to love other persons. We shall have more to say later on about the meaning of love as it applies to God. For the moment, it need only be said that the Christian perspective on reality is such that God is he who in his dealings with mankind, and above all his dealings with us through Jesus Christ, is the supreme instance of concern, self-giving for others. To find oneself in the position of being unavoidably involved in this particular kind of concern is to realize that to try to give an account of ultimate reality otherwise than in personal terms is quite out of the question.

3.2.2.3 We are not here attempting to give an exhaustive list of characteristics of personality; rather we are trying to mention one or two of the major indications of personality. We therefore mention only one further characteristic. It would be tempting to say that evidence of mind indicates presence of personality. But the amazing achievements of computer science and the possibilities opening up before cybernetics must serve as a warning here: a computer is a kind of mind but does not (unless it is a highly eccentric or faulty computer) have personality. Therefore it is preferable to choose as a final indicator of personality the existence of will.

Perhaps it might be thought that our previous reference to 'concern' in God would make the further singling out of 'will' superfluous. It is true that 'concern' does imply the presence of will; a mere machine can have concern for nothing. But it is worth mentioning separately as an indicator of personality because it enables us to make explicit certain things about the Christian interpretation of reality which might otherwise remain in the background. For to do justice to Christian experience of reality it is essential that God should not be spoken of statically, not just as being this or that, or having this or that quality or attribute, but dynamically, as doing certain things, acting in a certain way, not out of any inner necessity of nature but by a free exercise of will. If justice is to be done to some of the central affirmations of the Gospel, for example: 'The Word became flesh; he came to dwell among us' (John 1.14); 'But Christ died for us while we were yet sinners, and that is God's own proof of his love towards us' (Rom. 5.8) – then we are compelled to speak in some such terms as 'action' or 'event', and not just random, fortuitous action and event at that, but action and event controlled by will. We get at who God is through what he has willed to do. The corollary to this is that to be in tune with reality is not so much to see or understand things in a correct way as to respond in terms of living to the pressures of an ultimate will upon us. Similarly, to be out of tune with reality can be described with uncomfortable accuracy in terms of disobedience to this same will. To be 'found', 'reconciled', 'accepted', these are the kind of terms the Christian feels himself compelled to employ in his account of reality, and he would be denying an essential part of his experience if he conceded that there was anything either accidental or automatic about the process. He must go on to say that it happens by design, on purpose, as the fulfilment of an initiating act of loving will. This is the clearest possible justification for asserting that God is personal or even that reality is personality controlled by will.

3.3 No definition of God has so far been offered, nor any definition of personality in the modern psychological sense. But we have tried to show that some of the essential features of reality as experienced by the Church in its living interpretation of the Gospel are quite definite indications of personality, so much so as to justify adherence to the personal model in our thought about God. 'Personality' in this sense has become an essential category for our description of God because it sums up, integrates and holds together so many of the things we want to say about God. At the same time, it does not do violence to the way we actually think and feel and experience.

We have to ask, now, however, whether as much can be said of the older, logical language of personality in God, of God in three 'persons'. It is common knowledge that for many men and women today Trinitarian language is far more of a stumbling block than an aid to clear thought. 'Three into one won't go', as every schoolboy knows; traditional formulae about the Son being begotten of the Father and the Spirit proceeding from the Father and the Son – to many people such language only obscures the essential questions of the existence and nature of God. It is not difficult to appreciate that in another day, in another thought-world, this older, logical notion of personality did in its way perform a useful summative role, holding together in its way various aspects of reality which required to be integrated. But too many Christians are now so baffled with this manner of speaking, which does not actively tie in with the way they think and speak in other contexts, that we have seriously to ask whether it should not now deliberately and with a clear conscience be abandoned. In other words, we have to ask if there is any connection between our use of the word personality in the older logical sense – Personality in God – and our use of the same word in the modern psychological sense – Personality of God. If there were no such connection, then clarity would seem to demand that we abandon the use of personality in one of these two senses, finding another word and way of saying what needs to be said. But is it so?

3.3.1 Personality in the older sense means that in God there are three *personae* or modes of existence. In the more modern sense, it is used as a general description of the whole of the Godhead. These two senses cannot be combined so as to affirm that there are three personalities in the Godhead: no one would want to suggest that the separate *personae*, Father, Son and Holy Spirit, have separate self-consciousness or wills. That would obviously be a clear case of category mistake. But it is possible to say something of the relation between personality in God and personality of God.

3.3.1.1 Perhaps the simplest way of putting it is that personality in God is the basis of personality of God. We have already noted that in the past, theologians have been known to draw a distinction between God as he is in himself and God as he is in his relations with us, as he appears to us or is experienced by us. But this can be dangerous: for unless we could be sure that there was some essential connection between the two, then faith and our knowledge of God would be placed in jeopardy. God might only appear to us to be personal, trustworthy, but in reality, in himself, he might be something quite different, vengeful or, even worse, loftily indifferent. So while there must be no shrinking from saying that there is a great deal we do not know about God, depths of love, mystery and holiness which human minds may not fathom, yet the Christian view of reality is such that there is no final separation between God as he appears to us and God as he is in himself.

3.3.1.2 Now we have seen that we are justified in speaking of the personality of God because the data of his dealings with us provided ample indicators to enable us to do so. But unless we are going to be content to imply that only in his dealings with us does he appear to be personal and leave open the suggestion that apart from us, in himself, he might be something quite impersonal – on the model of a self-programming computer, shall we say? – then more needs to be said. It is this 'more' that the older teaching of the *personae*, personality in God, seeks to provide. Quite apart from his dealings with his creatures, God is life, in the fullest sense, love, in the supreme sense; in himself there is mutuality, togetherness, communication. All these terms life, love, mutuality, togetherness, communication, are relational terms, implying relationship between two or more subjects. The older teaching of '*personae*', God in three persons, Father, Son and Holy Spirit, provided precisely the framework within which such language could be used, a framework which concentration solely on the personality *of* God cannot provide, but a framework which is necessary to give full currency to what needs to be said of the personality of God. Such a framework, in whatever language it is expressed (we are not tied to any one language or system of logical categories), cannot, therefore, be dispensed with. Personality in God is in fact the presupposition, the basis of the personality of God. We shall see in the next chapter how it also helps us to avoid the mistake of concluding that because God is personal, he must therefore be a giant in the sky.

4 We have attempted in this chapter to indicate the ways in which the data for Christian understanding of reality seem, despite some dangers, to compel us to say first and foremost of God that he is personal. There is a further consideration which is relevant, indeed for many people, decisive, but which we have kept for the end of this chapter on the ground that strictly speaking it follows, rather than precedes, all that has been said so far. This concerns the manner of our encounter with God and the way in which we know him.

In the first chapter it was pointed out that God, as ultimate reality, is not to be thought of as one thing among many, or even one person among many. He is not available for objective inspection or experimentation and can therefore never become an object for scientific study. He has to do not with one isolatable part of reality or experience, but with all experience and the whole of reality. We cannot dig him out and dissect him, nor put him under a microscope or at the end of a telescope. Rather, he it is who encounters us, confronts us, challenges us, gives himself to us. One of the most fruitful insights of theology in recent years has been the realization that to know him is to know a 'Thou' rather than an 'It'. This is surely one of the clearest characteristics of a personal relationship, the 'I–Thou' relationship as it has been called with such general acceptance ever since the Jewish philosopher, Martin Buber, published his extraordinary little book, *I and Thou*.[1] This way of looking at things has helped us to acknowledge that our relationship with God, while unique, has much more in common with our knowledge of other persons than with our knowledge of other things. The appropriate attitude is not one of cool detachment, but involves our whole selves, our emotions, our intellect, our wills. He is to be responded to rather than studied, 'addressed' rather than 'expressed', worshipped and obeyed and adored, rather than talked about or used. In short, God is known as personal, through and through.

5   The manner in which God is known, then, no less than what is known of him, makes it imperative for us to hold on to the personal model in our speech about God. This is the first and most important thing that needs to be said. If ultimate reality is personal, then the consequences in terms of appropriate response to reality as expressed in everyday attitudes and actions are immense. But though to acknowledge that what is really real is personal takes us a long way, of itself it does not take us the whole way, and in subsequent chapters we have to find suitable qualifiers to give meaningful content to this personal reality. One of the reasons why recent writers have been suspicious of the personal model is that it appears inseparable from some other specific notion of a person – a benevolent dictator, a tired old man, a master

craftsman. But there is no reason why to speak of God as personal should entail enslavement to any such one notion. On the contrary, new ages have to find their own ways of making the personal model more precise, and it is interesting to note the suggestion that in a computerized, business–efficiency age, the idea of 'manager' might be put to good theological use! However that may be, the conclusion of this chapter must be that ultimate reality, God himself, is rightly known and to be spoken of not as 'What' but as 'Who'.

NOTES

1. Published in German in 1923, in English in 1937.

3 God as 'What'

1 Our conclusion thus far is that the Christian experience and understanding of the reality that is God is such that the first thing to be said is that it is personal. The data of what ultimately matters oblige us to keep the personal model in our speech about God. Moreover, the concept of personality is useful, in that it enables us to hold together and see, as it were, from a single unified perspective, various aspects of the matter which might otherwise appear unrelated, even at odds with each other. If we want to use such ideas as commitment, concern, acceptance, or of will or reconciliation, then to think of God as personal is natural, convincing and right. But before trying to put more content into this notion of God as personal, we must look at certain obvious objections which can be made against insistence on the priority of the personal model.

1.1 The first objection is posed by the question: is not the attempt to speak of God as primarily personal merely an unsophisticated, not to say crude, survival of primitive thinking, born of a particularly vicious and persistent blend of human fear, conceit, and wishful thinking? Time was when all the trappings of nature, the sun, moon and stars, the corn seed and the soil, the wind and the waves and the tempest were all endowed by the primitive mind with human or semi-human or super-human characteristics. But we know better now and would never dream of going back to what has been left far behind. In the same way, instead of clinging obstinately and, it may be, fearfully to a view of reality as personal, would it not be better to use some of the insights of the civilized Greeks, for example, and speak of 'the Highest Good'? Or to adopt the terminology of the great philosophers of the eighteenth and nineteenth centuries and speak rather of 'Absolute Spirit'? Or indeed to follow some twentieth-century theologians who opt for 'Being itself' or simply 'Ultimate Reality'?

1.2 The second objection is that already alluded to (see p. 37). 'Personal' seems automatically to imply 'a person', and from 'a person' it is only one short step to the Big Person, who has become such an embarrassment to contemporary theology. Men have become increasingly aware that the alleged existence of such a person, dwelling in his own private space, thinking his own inscrutable thoughts, with his own inhuman or super-human attributes, is at best an irrelevance to human life and reality and at worst an intolerable threat. Hence the call by the most sensitive of current authors on this point to 'depersonify but not to depersonalize'.[1]

1.3 These objections are legitimate and serious and require more by way of an answer than a defiant 'Here I stand – I can do no other'. But however sensitive we are to them, we do no service to truth or reality if we allow them to make us abandon the personal model as our primary insight into reality. The exasperated, hen-pecking wife may well feel justified, after reeling off a rich catalogue of the points wherein her wretched husband falls short of her idea of humanity, in her conclusion: 'Why, you're not a man at all!' But the husband can hardly be expected to share in this conclusion. No more can the Christian allow himself to be persuaded by an exhaustive list of points wherein God must differ from a human being, to conclude that he is not personal after all.

2 The irony of the situation is that something like this can all too easily happen and has in fact happened. When Christian thinkers and systematizers were seeking to find a suitable 'reality framework' into which to fit their own special insights and intuitions, nothing like the modern notion of personality was available to them. All they had was a highly sophisticated, highly impersonal picture of reality in which what ultimately mattered was the non-worldly, the non-human, the non-personal. This was the Aristotelian metaphysic of substance, which dominated all the thinking and categorizing and creed-making of the fathers of the Church in the early centuries of Christendom. It was also a high-precision version of this same metaphysic that was rediscovered by the doctors of the Church in the late Middle Ages and which received its normative Christian form in the teachings of Thomas Aquinas. Furthermore, it was this same metaphysical framework which survived the sixteenth-century Reformation, and remained standard for orthodoxy, Catholic and Protestant, unreformed and reformed, in their heydays.

2.1 This metaphysical framework made it virtually impossible to start with the question, 'Who is God?' It presupposed that God is a 'what', to be described by contrast with the human condition and characterized by absence of anything that might savour of the imperfections of humanity and the world men know. The world and life in the world was finite, temporal, contingent, relative: therefore God must be infinite, eternal, absolute; the world and life in the world was all change, decay, coming into existence and going out of existence; therefore God must be unchanging (immutable), incorruptible, impassible (incapable of being altered or affected from without). Thus God was to be thought of as a thing-like, static perfection, a trellis, or even a tailor's dummy on which could be hung various attributes – infinite, eternal, absolute, immutable, impassible and so on.

God as this thing-like being, whom all men, Christian or not, could conceive by the simple if strenuous exercise of reason, was that with which the God of Christian revelation had to be equated. When Christians wanted to speak the good news of the God of love, the Father of their Lord Jesus Christ, they had to use the only mental tools at their disposal, the equipment provided by this common metaphysical framework. So the decisive things they wanted to say to express their community experience of God who not only created the world but acted in righteousness, forgiveness and self-giving love to redeem and love and sustain it, had to be expressed as further attributes which could be fitted on to the existing, partly-clad frame. The list which began with infinite, eternal, etc., is now extended by the addition of wisdom, righteousness, power, goodness, truth and so on.

2.2 The problem inevitably arose as to how the various attributes were to be reconciled with each other. How was goodness (which implied forgiveness) to be reconciled with righteousness or justice (which demanded non-forgiveness)? How were the moral attributes (wisdom, righteousness, goodness, etc.) to be reconciled with others which seemed to rule out the possibility of moral action (unchangeable, impassible)? This problem of reconciliation was usually solved by resorting to the contention that God's goodness, for example, was not to be equated with human goodness, so that what appeared to be a *prima facie* contradiction in human terms was not so when it was a question of the goodness of God. Further, God's revelation of himself to humanity (attributes relating to the divine operations) was, as it were, specially adapted for reception by finite, fallible human minds for the express purpose of salvation, but in reality the infinite, eternal world of spirit in which God dwelt was so different from the finite temporal world of matter in which men and women lived that what God seemed to be in the latter was not in fact what he was in the former (attributes relating to God's being). God in himself was not what God appeared to be in his revelation to the world.

2.3 It is extremely difficult, well-nigh impossible for us to get inside the thought-world which expressed its knowledge of reality in this way. All we can do is make a sympathetic effort to understand and, more important, frankly acknowledge that this strange framework was indeed sufficient to sustain life, worship, devotion and compassion for many centuries. There are good grounds for believing that only by breaking out of this particular metaphysical framework could mankind make great new advances in science, could new insights into the nature of man and human behaviour emerge, and new understanding of reality, of God, come to light. Nevertheless, an anxious, uncertain generation can hardly criticize their ancestors for holding to a view of reality which for all its present obscurities and inconsistencies yet provided a backdrop of certainty and serenity against which men's lives were to be lived.

2.3.1 The fact remains, however, that it is no more possible for us to see reality in that kind of framework, with those kinds of categories, than it is for us, when sick, to resort to the primitive medicines which the mediaeval doctors would prescribe. If we try to do so, practical schizophrenia is the inevitable outcome, as one view of reality has to be 'put on', as it were, when we speak of God and our relation to him, and quite another view of reality presupposed in every other sphere of living or thought. Worse still, the 'what'-God of static substance and innumerable attributes, when identified with the irrepressibly active 'who'-God of the Bible and Christian experience, acquires the life of an alien giant in an alien sky. These various attributes which served to protect this being from the appearance of a mere human being, writ however large, now operate to take away the characteristics which might help us to understand its being as truly personal. Who ever heard of an 'immutable' person, or 'impassible' love? Once the giant-in-the-sky picture is arrived at, the effect of loading on to it the attributes of the 'what'-God is not to make it more accurate and credible, but to obscure it to the point of meaningless. It dies, as has been said in another connexion, the death of a thousand qualifications.

2.3.2 What, then, is to be made of the time-honoured fruits of a 'what'-God theology? Enough was said in the last chapter to indicate that the 'God-as-who' approach is justified and must constitute our starting point. Does this mean that the older view must simply now be abandoned to the scrap heap of error of the past? This is indeed a temptation, and one to which many modern philosophers and theologians have succumbed. But it is often a desperate expedient, and not a little arrogant as well, to assume that the great thinkers of the past were all wrong, not in general only but in every particular as well. Neither honour nor wisdom bids us start with a completely clean sheet. So what is to be made of the attributes of the 'what'-God of old?

3 The older theology of orthodoxy (Protestant and Catholic) knew many classifications of the divine attributes. For example, attributes which relate to God's being (e.g. simplicity, truth, goodness, infinity), attributes which relate to the divine operations (e.g. wisdom, providence; love, with mercy and justice; omnipotence) or attributes of him who is the embodiment of all perfection and intelligence (e.g. happiness, beauty, holiness). Or again, another well-recognized classification of the attributes was to divide them into the incommunicable attributes (e.g. simplicity, infinity, immutability) and the communicable attributes (e.g. life, understanding, will, goodness, justice, freedom, power). But the classification which may prove to be the most useful to us is that which put the divine attributes into four groups: those which equally qualify all the rest (e.g. infinite, absolute, immutable); natural attributes (e.g. spirit, self-existence, eternity, freedom of will, intelligence, power); moral attributes (e.g. righteousness, goodness, truth and faithfulness); and 'the beauty of holiness as the consummate glory of all the divine perfections in union'. This last classification is useful not because of the details of the distribution but because it recognizes a class of attributes which equally qualify all the rest. This does offer a way of utilizing some of the insights of the older static 'what'-God theology without having to resort to nonsense, silence or total obscurity or to abandon the personal model. For it enables us usefully to re-interpret at least some of the traditional attributes, not as abstractions and as décor of a static figure but as qualifiers to help us to develop in an accurate way whatever models the data may have suggested to us. Four examples of the possible re-deployment of traditional attributes will here suffice to illustrate the point.

3.1 Traditionally, 'infinity' was a contrast term, used to indicate how God differed in his essence from men and the world of men. Perhaps the most obvious thing that can be said about our world is that everything in it is finite: it has a beginning and an end, it is limited by all sorts of conditions. We live, we grow old, we die. What we do depends, among other things, on where we happen to be, how much we happen to know, what means we have at our disposal, who our parents are and so on. In short, we are finite, as is everything that we can see, hear, touch and feel. By contrast, God is to be thought of as not subject to any of these limitations, and therefore as infinite.

3.1.1 So far so good, and so innocuous as well. But when we pause to consider what we have so far done in speaking of God as 'infinite', trouble arises. For one thing, it must be said that in speaking this way we may have succeeded in saying something negative about man (what man is not), but we have not necessarily succeeded in saying anything positive about God. For another thing, while it is possible to understand what is intended by saying that God is not finite in this or that particular respect – with regard to space, or knowledge or ability – it is highly questionable whether gathering this all up into one abstract concept of infinity which is then predicated of God really means anything at all. Certainly 'the Infinite' of philosophical speculation is not the personal God of Christian faith. Worst of all, because the very word 'infinite' for many people has predominantly a spatial association, the word on its own suggests the idea of super-size, 'gigantic-plus', as it were, spacelessness beyond space. This would bring us back again to the giant beyond the sky, at least the un-philosophical among us. For the philosophical, it leads straight to contradiction.

3.1.2 If these consequences are to be avoided, it is necessary to be more precise. This can best be done by using the notion 'infinite', not to denote some attribute which of itself can be ascribed to some person or thing but to qualify another adjective; by using it adverbially, in other words, rather than adjectivally. We shall not say, then, that God is infinite. But we shall say that God is 'infinitely' this or that, loving, for example, or gracious. This means that 'infinite' is being used to qualify other things we want to say about God, it will function as indicating the direction in which these other things we want to say are to be developed. This is what we mean by a 'qualifier'.

3.1.2.1 How, then, will this work? We can start by acknowledging that the philosophers of old who developed this term were not as naïve as has sometimes been portrayed. Even in the Middle Ages, a distinction was made between a 'true infinite' and a 'false infinite'. The false infinite was a quantitative notion, that is to say it related to amount or intensity. It would appear as the end term of a series such as the following: A is good, B is fairly good, C is rather good, D is very good, E is extremely good . . . Z is infinitely good. But 'good' always implies 'better' so that 'infinitely good' cannot be a repository for the ultimate in goodness. Viewed from this perspective it must be meaningless. A 'true infinite' on the other hand, was no mere quantitative prolongation of the finite to the highest possible degree but rather qualitatively different. This can be illustrated with a simple mathematical example. Take the series

$$1, 1+\frac{1}{2}, 1+\frac{1}{2^2}, 1+\frac{1}{2}+\frac{1}{2^2}+\frac{1}{2^3} \ldots, 1+\frac{1}{2}+\frac{1}{2^2} \ldots \frac{1}{2^{n-1}}$$

This series could be indefinitely extended but however nearly it might approach the number 2 it will never reach it. Yet it is not out of relation to the number 2. It is, rather, 'a number outside the series and of a different logical status altogether from the terms of the series, but a number which may be said to preside over and label the whole sequence of ever-expanding sums'.[2] In a similar way, 'infinite' is not unrelated to 'finite' but it indicates not simply an indefinite extension or the greatest imaginable intensity but rather a difference in quality. This is how it works when it qualifies whatever we wish to say about God.

3.1.2.2 'Infinity', then, can no longer intelligibly be understood as something which God 'has' and creation, man and nature, lacks. Rather it is used adverbially to make more precise certain ways of speaking of God. For example, 'infinite' and 'loving' are not two separate aspects of the matter. He is not 'infinite' and then, also, 'loving'. If we say he is 'infinite' and add nothing more, we have really said nothing at all. But if we see 'infinite' as not describing something he is but as indicating the way in which he is certain other things, then it can still be meaningful. We said it was to be used adverbially, and we meant by this that the appropriate use of a word like 'infinite' is in such a phrase as 'infinitely loving'. 'Loving', here, invites us to recall all we mean by human love. 'Infinitely', the qualifier, invites us to develop our thoughts of human love in such a way that we come to see that God is loving in a way not unrelated to what we mean by love among human persons but in such a way that compels us to speak of a difference of quality rather than a mere increase in quantity or intensity. For the Christian, of course, this process of developing a model ('loving') in a certain direction ('infinitely') is not an arbitrary or subjective process. It is demanded and controlled by the data of what ultimately matters. In other words, we allow Jesus Christ to put content into what we mean by God as loving.

3.1.3 We shall investigate this more fully later on (see pp. 83 ff.). In the meantime we may summarize. 'Infinite' as applied to God does not make sense on its own. But combined with some other adjective it can help to develop the description in a true and helpful way, so that there is a reliable disclosure of reality, even if it cannot be fully put into words. We looked briefly at the phrase 'infinitely loving'. This phrase is justified because it evokes and sums up the situation of the Christian when he finds himself echoing St Paul with his persuasion that literally nothing can separate him from the love of God which is in Christ Jesus (Rom. 8.38 f.).

3.2 We can present our second illustration much more briefly, as the traditional attribute we are dealing with now operates in much the same way as 'infinite'. This is *'eternal'*.

One might have thought that this adjective simply indicates that God is not subject to the limitations of time; another contrast word, to claim that unlike us, God does not have a certain life span which has a beginning in time, lasts for a certain time and ends in time. Unlike us, he is not subject to the ravages of time, growing up, growing old, incapable of falling out of its onward march except by death. 'Eternal' does indicate all this, but in the past, it has been used to indicate much more.

3.2.1 Long and fierce the philosophical battles have raged over the meaning of eternity. If God is not subject to the kind of time we are subject to, in what kind of time (='eternity') does he 'dwell'? The notion of eternity was abstracted from other things that could be said of God, conceptualized as an attribute, one more with which to clothe the divine frame, and 'eternity' became something God 'had' or 'in which he dwelt'. Discussion then centred, and indeed still does, on what this concept of eternity, when applied to God, could mean. Is it an infinite extension of the time we know, both backwards and forwards? Is it timeless-ness? Or is it a special kind of time, God's time, different from our time but about which, save that it is not our time, we can, by definition, know nothing? Or is it a mode of existence, transcending the temporal altogether, to which all experience is not successive but simultaneous or 'compresent'?

Such questions give some idea of the complexity of the area in which we are now treading. We need not, however, involve ourselves too deeply, except to acknowledge that each of the answers hinted at is fraught with philosophical difficulties, especially if the concept of eternity which results is conjoined with the notion of a living, active God. But this by no means obliges us to abandon this term. It only suggests that, like 'infinite', it may be more usefully employed in a different way.

3.2.2 Like 'infinite', it can serve as a qualifier of certain other things which can be said of God. Like 'infinite' it suggests quality rather than quantity. Whatever God is, he is in an 'untemporary' way. He is not now this, now that and tomorrow who knows what. Whatever we know him to be, he can be relied on to be. Thus he can be spoken of meaningfully as 'eternally purposeful', 'eternally righteous', 'eternally loving'. On the whole, the highly figurative language of worship of the Bible is to many people of more help in communicating the eternal-ness of God than the abstracting efforts of philosophy and theology. 'Behold, He that keepeth Israel shall neither slumber nor sleep' (Ps. 121.4); 'A thousand years in Thy sight are but as yesterday when it is past' (Ps. 90.4); 'Thy kingdom is an everlasting kingdom' (Ps. 145.13); 'Underneath are the everlasting arms' (Deut. 33.27); 'To God only wise, be glory through Jesus Christ for ever' (Rom. 16.27); 'This is life eternal, that they might know thee and the only true God, and Jesus Christ, whom thou hast sent' (John 17.3).

This last reference, from St John's Gospel, provides a very useful illustration of the use of 'eternal' as a qualifier. For here, 'eternal life' is not to be understood either as an unending extension of the life of time now known, nor as a completely new existence which begins at death, but rather as a new quality of existence which begins here and now in this life of time, the main characteristic of which is awareness of inseparability from the knowledge and love of God.

3.3 'Infinite' and 'eternal' are familiar members of the Christian vocabulary, and have a time-honoured place, particularly in the language in which God is addressed in prayer. We have tried to show that when understood as qualifiers rather than as attributes, they still have a meaningful place in that vocabulary. The next traditional term we consider presents even sharper difficulties: the 'immutability' of God.

3.3.1 In one sense, of course, it presents no difficulty. The Christian view of reality is such that when Christians think of God who addresses them in Christ, they think of him as One whose purpose does not change, who can be relied upon, whose constancy is certain (e.g. Ex. 3.14; Mal. 3.6; Ps. 102.25 ff.; James 1.17; Heb. 6.13–18). Trouble arises, however, when the personal model fades into the background and the 'what'-God dominates the scene. Now 'immutability' no longer refers to some aspect of God's being – his purpose, or faithfulness, or trustworthiness or love – but becomes a separate attribute, something God 'has'. As such it assumes a key role, and any qualification of it can only be interpreted as raising a question against the supremacy and majesty of God. A 'what'-God, to be perfect, must be immutable 'in himself', subject to no change or movement. This may help to suggest an exalted principle or substance, but it makes it logically impossible to talk meaningfully about God entering into relation in creation, or loving, or forgiving. Strict immutability would rule this out. Christian theologians, operating with a 'what'-like concept of God, as they attempted to do justice to the data of reality, were forced to resort to dangerous distinctions in order to introduce the specifically Christian insights at all. So they postulated a difference between 'God as he is in himself', who was indeed immutable, and God in his dealings with creation, of whom they allowed a limited mutability. This was hardly satisfactory.

3.3.2 Even less satisfactory is the straight transfer of this idea of immutability from its proper context of 'what'-God to the context of 'who'-God, where the personal model predominates. For it simply does not make sense to try to say 'God is personal – and he is also immutable'. Whatever else it implies, 'personal' must involve a constant growth and development of relationships – love, forgiveness, communication, response – all of which would be ruled out by a strict application of immutability. Does this mean, then, that if the 'God as what' concept gives way to that of 'God as who', immutability and all its works must be entirely abandoned?

3.3.3 Not necessarily. Once again, if we understand it strictly as a qualifier of something else, it can still be usefully employed as truly reflecting certain aspects of the data. It can point to God's self-consistency and help us to affirm that he cannot cease to be himself, either in himself or in relation to his creatures (see Ex. 3.14). He is not unchangeable by virtue of some external law of necessity. As personal, he wills it. And so, unlike a human being, his virtues are not subject to change by death, or degeneration, or vacillation, ignorance or fear. Furthermore, we can see it as an entirely appropriate qualifier of God's love. To be sure, 'immutable love' is an odd-sounding phrase but it can be helpful and true if we understand it to indicate the absolute constancy and utter reliability of God's love. This is precisely what the Christian community wants to affirm of reality when it acknowledges the complete decisiveness of God's action in Christ. It does not mean that God has to act towards his creation in a uniform way. If God has given freedom in any sense to his creatures then his immutable purpose of love towards them demands that he also is free to act and re-act in ways appropriate to their action. So even as a qualifier, 'immutable' is misleading, indeed erroneous, if it in any way implies lifelessness, or the immutability of death. But it is used usefully and correctly if it speaks rather of constant vitality, in dynamic rather than static terms.

3.3.4 This is no mere quibbling over words. Unless immutability is purged of associations of lifelessness, or utter immobility, it makes impossible a specifically Christian understanding of God. For, as we have seen, in this understanding the place of Jesus is decisive. But if God is immutable in the sense of being completely static, unchangeably solid or single, it becomes a meaningless contradiction to speak in terms of incarnation, of Word made flesh or God made man. On the other hand, the dynamic way of speaking of immutability becomes not only possible but necessary, if justice is to be done to all that Christians want to say of the divine action in incarnation and reconciliation. For this is not understood as a fortuitous afterthought on the part of God, as if, for example, it had been necessary as emergency action to counteract the failure of human beings to live the kind of lives for which they were created. Rather it is understood as the furthering and fulfilment of God's purpose, his immutable purpose to give himself to his creatures and reconcile them with himself. He does not become someone he was not before: he remains himself. So, too, his purpose remains unchanging. This is what makes it possible for unqualified reliance to be placed on him.

3.4 Finally let us consider one further traditional description of God which has loomed far larger in Christian and non-Christian philosophical discussion than it has in the practical world of Christian worship. What can be meant by speaking of God as 'Absolute'? This is the attribute par excellence of the 'what'-God, the ultimate in everything this world and its inhabitants are not. As such, it figures prominently in many concepts of God, both in the Western philosophical tradition and in certain Oriental religions. Hegel's famous exposition of reality as 'Absolute Spirit' is the most influential example of the former, while the Hindu idea of God is the most important instance of the latter.

3.4.1 To talk of the 'what'-God as absolute certainly makes sense. It effectively conveys that such a God is conditioned in no way at all, utterly independent of anything or anyone that is, uncontaminated by anything relative, untouched, even, by anything else, pure passivity, perfect in isolation, unmoving and unmoved. It also, however, very effectively conveys that such a God is the very antithesis of personal. To speak of such a God as creating, entering into relationship with his creation and enjoying and being enjoyed by his creatures would be sheer contradiction. Oil and water is a more plausible mixture than God as 'the Absolute' and God as Love.

3.4.2 If we are to hold to the personal model, then in our thinking of God, 'absolute' as a separate attribute must go. But can it be retained and usefully employed as a qualifier, in the sense in which we have found employment for the other traditional attributes we have considered? In fact, if an adequate account is to be given of reality as experienced by the Christian community, it can be so employed. For in terms of that experience, God confronts us with a claim, a demand, an offer, a gift, all of which are qualified in no way whatever, contingent on nothing, so that 'absolute' is an entirely proper way of characterizing them. His authority, his commitment and concern, his salvation would likewise be highly questionable if we could not rely on them as being in the same way unconditional or absolute, and if, consequently, he did not require an unconditional response, an absolute commitment from those who claim to know him. In all these ways, it is proper to qualify the things we want to say of God by the description 'absolute'. Furthermore, it is worth adding that certain attempts at definition of God are really definitions in terms of absoluteness. Paul Tillich, for example, has made sense for many people by defining God as 'our ultimate concern'; and if we prefer to hold to a more personal way of speaking and define God as 'He with whom we have to do', this is still a definition in absolute terms.

3.4.3 To avoid misunderstanding, it would be as well to say explicitly that although we can find useful employment for the term 'absolute' in the way that has been suggested, the data will not allow us to use this word 'absolute' if it in any way implies the isolation or non-relatedness of God to the world or ourselves. Such an implication has often been encouraged, with the intention, presumably, of safeguarding the point that while man and his universe are totally dependent on God, God is in no way dependent on man or on the universe. He does not need them, as it were, to enable him to exist as God. There is truth here, but it needs careful handling if its insight is not to be converted into a frightening impression of apathy or divine indifference to the world and the affairs of the world. We shall return to this point later. For the moment, it will be sufficient to affirm that in using this word 'absolute' as a qualifier we are not implying an absence of relationship between God and everything that is not God. He is not relative to the world, but he is related to it in the closest possible way, 'absolutely related',[3] to everything that is.

4 In the last chapter, we saw that the data for a Christian understanding of reality were such as to make it imperative to start with the personal model; in this chapter, we have been looking at what seems to have been the natural tendency in philosophy and in certain religions to think of God as a 'what' instead of as a 'who', to start with an impersonal instead of a personal model. We have also seen that when language appropriate to the personal model is merely tacked on to the language appropriate to the impersonal model, some distinctly odd, indeed sometimes contradictory results emerge. Clarity is not served by starting with an idea or thing-like substance or principle of which one predicates such impersonal attributes as infinite, eternal, immutable, absolute, and then continuing by adding on such personal attributes as loving, merciful and just. It is, however, not only possible but positively helpful, in terms of our data, to see some of the traditional 'what'-God attributes as appropriate qualifiers of the personal model. Such a procedure, we contend, serves the dual purpose of qualifying the personal model so as to get away from the cruder representation of God as a giant in the sky and of avoiding the 'death of a thousand qualifications' which would result from a mere piling on of innumerable attributes drawn indiscriminately from the personal and the impersonal realms.

NOTES

1. J. A. T. Robinson, *Exploration into God* (London: SCM Press; California: Stanford University Press, 1967), p. 87.

2. This example is taken from I. T. Ramsey, *Religious Language* (London: SCM Press; New York: The Macmillan Company, 1957), pp. 69 f.

3. To use the language of Charles Hartshorne in his interesting study, *The Divine Relativity* (New Haven: Yale University Press, 1948).

4 Up, Down, In and Around

1 We have just been seeing how some of the attributes traditionally ascribed to 'God as what' might be taken over for service in relation to 'God as who' if they were employed as qualifiers of the personal model. God is not infinite but infinitely loving, not eternal but eternally life-bestowing, not absolute but absolutely related to everything that is. We now turn to another traditional attribute, to 'transcendence', to see if it can be employed in the same way. It deserves separate treatment, because it will introduce us to the bewildering but perfectly proper question, 'Where is God?'

2 When Yuri Gagarin returned from his pioneer flight round the world in outer space, he announced, with great good humour, that he had seen no sign of God. It was a good joke. Significantly, it was enjoyed as much by Christian believers as by dedicated atheists. Even more significantly, it was resented by no serious Christians, for whom it was so wide of the mark, so unrelated to anything that they really believed, that it was in no way offensive. This could be interpreted as the most convincing evidence possible that no Christian, at least, thinks of God as a physical being to be located, not to say bumped into, in outer space. For God is spirit, and whatever else that may mean for Christians it means that he can never be thought of as a physical or quasi-physical object.

2.1 If then he is not a physical object to be located in outer space, where is he? We are often told that the traditional belief is that he 'dwells' ('lives', for some odd reason, is avoided) in some non-physical 'space' beyond the physical universe of men and matter. In this 'space' he was, apparently, thought to exist in splendid isolation from the world or universe that men know. This was his proper habitation, to which men of faith hoped to go when they died, thereby escaping through faith and the merits of Christ from this transient world and vale of woe to their eternal home with God. In relation to this present world, God's interest, if not purely coincidental, was at least limited to condemning it and getting men out of it. God was, in effect, alienated from it, an alien God. Certainly no Christian today would recognize this alien God, though the impression that something like this was the traditional view is so widespread that, on the doubtful principle of 'no smoke without fire', presumably it does embody some elements of what Christians have believed in the past. Possibly something like it developed as insights into the nature of God as personal gave way to impersonal thinking, and the unhealthy and illogical amalgam of 'God as who' and 'God as what' emerged.

2.2 This idea of an alienated God can, of course, easily be repudiated by a quick reference to the data. The biblical witness to the God and Father of Jesus Christ is unambiguous. Without quoting pages of available texts, it would surely be agreed that the Old Testament witness is to God as active in the world, as having created all things and remaining Lord of all things, as shewing a peculiar concern for the people of Israel, and that not for their own sakes but for the sake of all 'nations'. The central affirmations of the New Testament develop these Old Testament emphases to maximum pitch by proclaiming the man Jesus as the Logos or Word of God coming 'unto his own': God in Christ, reconciling the world to himself, freeing all men for life in conformity with the living truth which is God. The basic conviction of the Church throughout the centuries, even in its most disreputable periods, has been that Christian faith is a living response to God who is attentive, caring and active in this world. Common sense tells men now, as it has always done, that if what goes on in this world here and now is of no interest to God, then he cannot have had anything to do with Jesus, nor have anything to do with anyone else, present or past.

3   That this 'alien God' view has little enough to do with Christian faith should, then, be obvious. How it can ever have been thought otherwise would be a mystery but for one thing: it testifies – in an absurdly exaggerated degree – to one aspect of the matter which Christians would always want to hold on to. This is what is traditionally called the *transcendence* of God, the acknowledgment that God is not to be exhaustively identified with the whole or any part or parts of the universe and what goes on in it. In all that he is, he goes beyond or transcends anything that may correctly be said of men or nature.

3.1   The Bible has its own way of making this point. In it is not to be found any theological analysis of the concept of transcendence or any equivalent concept. But the fact of God's transcendence is to be reflected in the response of the men of the Bible to God, in their language of address to him, the language of devotion or praise or commitment. As such, the language is highly figurative, and effectively suggestive. 'My thoughts are not your thoughts, neither are your ways my ways, saith the Lord' (Isa. 55.8). 'The heaven of heavens cannot contain thee' (I Kings 8.27). So far does he transcend the goings-on and practical possibilities of this world, that reference to him can be made in crudely picturesque terms: 'He that sitteth in the heavens shall laugh' (Ps. 2.4) at human pretentiousness and self-conceit; what he has built he is in a position to demolish, as someone who has been trying his hand at pottery is in a position to shatter his creation to smithereens. God's goodness, his power, his greatness, go far beyond anything that men or nature can know. Biblical references to the divine transcendence could be multiplied, but the point has to be made at once that such references are never to be found in a neutral descriptive context. That is to say, they are never given as a detached answer to the question, 'Where is God?' or 'What is God like?' Instead, they are to be found as answers to questions like 'What does God require of us?' 'How shall

I give thanks for what he has done and is doing for us?' 'Where is Israel going wrong?' 'Whom can we trust?' 'What can we hope for?' 'What is my relation to my enemy?' 'Why did this have to happen?' In other words, God's transcendence is not used as providing a description of God: it is a necessary means of expressing adequate response, an indispensable component of a real reaction to reality.

3.2 Trouble only arises when men abstract from this situation of response and reflect on the conditions that must obtain to make it appropriate. There is nothing improper in this. It is natural and right that it should happen, that men should try to find expression for the truth. But it does create difficulties. In particular, it is difficult to isolate the component of acknowledging the 'beyondness' of God, which is an integral feature of response, and to express it as a theological concept. The source of the difficulty is obvious. If it were possible adequately and completely to express the beyondness of God, there would be at least one sense in which this beyondness would have to be denied, and that is in terms of human understanding. So, facing this difficulty, men have recognized the mystery of how God goes beyond human experience and qualities, and those attempts to present the divine transcendence in conceptual terms have been motivated by the hope not of dissolving the mystery but of defining it more precisely, and of indicating at least its direction and area.

3.3 Sometimes this has been forgotten, and the mystery has not been respected. Indeed, attempts have been made to dissolve it. This has happened whenever God's transcendence has been considered primarily in terms of size and space. The product of speculation along these lines has been the Gagarin-type expectation, and its consequence, eventually, has been the idea of an alien God. Conscious of the dangers of such an approach, and appreciating that however concise it might be as a logical construct it utterly failed to do justice to the Christian data and the Christian hope, Christian thinkers have, notably in our age, been trying to approach the transcendence of God in a radically different way. God as 'up there' or 'out there' has given way to God as 'the ground of our being', or as the 'man for others'. So-called metaphysical transcendence (an 'other-worldly transcendence) gives way to transcendence as 'historically conceived'.

3.4 This point may be expanded by looking for a moment at various answers that have been given to the question: 'Where are men to look for God?'

3.4.1.1 A metaphysical 'other world' interpretation of God's transcendence would lead to an answer in terms of some other world than the one we know: God is to be found in a heaven beyond, if not above the skies, beyond death. It would be wrong to imply that Christians in the past who have held to this interpretation have denied any relation between God in his heaven and this world of space and time. In so far as it was Christian at all, it always included some acknowledgment that God was active in this world, as creator in the first place, as Redeemer in Christ offering salvation from it, as ever present in the Church, his foothold on earth as it were, offering security from the dangerous distractions of this world, giving worth to present activity in this world as valuable preparation for future happiness with him in heaven. But the emphasis of this 'other-world' interpretation was clearly not primarily on transformation of life here and now: it was on being kept safe during life in this world so as to be fit for habitation in that other world after death.

3.4.1.2 That this interpretation sufficed as a framework within which the Christian message was expressed and Christian life lived may be accepted without too much difficulty. That it is now no longer adequate is equally obvious. The simplest reason for this is that it is just not intelligible to many people today. The deeper and better reason is that it does not seem adequate to the data of Christian faith. In particular, it does not enable the message of Incarnation to be taken with radical seriousness. If the Christian message is the message of Word made flesh, God made man, coming 'unto his own' and loving them to the last, then it must follow that God has accepted once and for all this world, which we know, as the object of his concern and the sphere of his operations. The idea of an 'other world' may or may not be meaningful: what has become increasingly clear is that if God is to be known at all it must be here and now in this life, in this world of space and time.

3.4.2 This conviction has led certain theologians to interpret God's transcendence in historical terms. Where is he to be looked for? In our own personal history, in the history we make ourselves, in our dealings, our encounter with other people. More particularly, God encounters us by confronting us in the event Jesus Christ, in judgment and grace, giving us a new understanding of ourselves, our neighbour, our place in our world and our God. He is to be encountered in the decisions that lie before us, in living situations great and small, dramatic and undramatic, in the challenge of other people without whom we cannot be persons, in the personal existence that is our opportunity. The traditional Jewish and Christian insight is that God acts in history. But what is now being said goes beyond this. God not only acts in history but exists for us in history. There is nothing arbitrary about this existence. For, it is further claimed, God exists for us 'not in the conceptual forms of the absolute, the metaphysical, infinite etc. . . . but the "man for others", and therefore the Crucified, the man who lives out of the transcendent'.[1]

3.4.2.1 Now it might be thought by an unsympathetic critic that all this is nothing but an elaborate, high-sounding way of saying that God is other people: that knowing and responding to other people is what we really mean by knowing and responding to God. God, in other words, is a synonym for co-humanity. But this would be a distortion of the view under discussion. It is, after all, trying to get at the transcendence of God from a new perspective, a perspective which does not need to alienate him to an 'other world'. It sees the reality of transcendence as an event which happens to us. It happens to me whenever I am confronted by another human being and encounter him not as a statistic, a pawn, or a talking thing, but as a person, whenever I am 'aware of the presence of another centre of will and of personal being',[2] whenever, to use the current jargon, I encounter another 'I' as a 'Thou' and he in his turn, encounters me as a 'Thou'. When that happens, something is experienced which is more than the sum total of the component parts of the two parties; a mysterious relation is set up. Such is transcendence. But in the other, the Thou, we encounter not only the other, the Thou, but God. He transcends history by encountering us in it. 'In the I–Thou relation we glimpse the eternal Thou.'[3] So his transcendence is 'the expression for the historical reality of his encounter with his creatures'.[4] The only being of God which Christians may speak of is his being for others.

It is in this being for others that the act of God is to be apprehended – not direct, not as a theophany or an objectifiable miracle, not comprehensible, not fully expressible – as the way of his love. We cannot get nearer to God than this: he is not accessible in isolation or in abstraction, as a being or as being itself. He is known only as he gives himself, and in this giving he expresses himself as entirely historical.[5]

3.4.2.2 God, then, according to this view, is to be found as he encounters us in our own history. In this encounter, he comes to us from beyond, taking the initiative, remaining himself, utterly other, even while he encounters us. But, it may particularly be asked, how is he to be recognized? How do we know it is God we are encountering and not just our own imagination or wishful thinking? In one sense, there is a check here provided by Jesus Christ. It is as we encounter him as he is proclaimed that we encounter God. But in another sense, because it is by faith that we know God, we have to run the risk of doing without any supports, props or proofs which could guarantee that it was in fact *God* we encountered. So sensitive have the proponents of this view become to the danger of returning to an 'other-world' God (other-worldly transcendence) that apart from God's encounter with us, there is apparently no possibility of saying anything positive about God as he is in himself.

All that we can say of the absolutely Other, of God, is that in his paradoxical giving of himself to us, which we receive in faith, the faith that we are forgiven and reconciled, we do indeed believe that it is not simply of ourselves and of the human other that we are speaking, but of God.[6]

3.5 Such is the attempt to get away from speaking of the otherness of God in 'other-world' terms, as metaphysical transcendence. What is suggested instead is that his otherness is to be experienced and expressed only in history, as historical transcendence. This is a difficult notion to grasp, and yet it is surely a great advance. For one thing, it enables Christians to be completely consistent in their doctrine of Incarnation. If God became man in Jesus Christ, this must mean that he has accepted this world of space and time as the proper area of his operations: that is where he is at work and that is where he is to be found. For another thing, it reinforces the insight which Christians have always acknowledged but which, with too much emphasis on otherworldliness and escape from this world, has not always been easy to express: namely, that the appropriate response to reality is in living, in living for and with other men and women, with 'fellowmen', as it has recently been put.[7] It allows the world of today with its massive problems and its fantastic possibilities to be taken with absolute seriousness because it is possible to acknowledge that it is here, and nowhere else, that what ultimately matters is to be found, or rather discloses itself.

3.6 This view of the transcendence of God as historical surely goes a long way to answer the suspicion of humanists that belief in a transcendent God must prejudice interest in man – his predicament, his possibility, his future – for the sake of doing obeisance to an alien God. With such a view, it is just not possible to believe or teach that concern for the present welfare and future prospects of fellow men is in any way subsidiary to self-preservation by opting out or by saving one's soul. The sphere of service of the Church can the more readily be seen as the secular world. To be in tune with reality therefore means to be committed without reserve to one's fellow man. That such notes should sound so clearly is surely great gain.

3.7 There are, however, difficulties in this view which it would be wrong and foolish to ignore. The only one relevant here is the objection that this view actually enables us to say very little about God. It allows us to say that he is other, that his transcendence is to be experienced in history and that, confronted as we are with the event of Jesus Christ, we encounter him in our encounter with others. But what, in effect, can we say about him who does the encountering? We are told it is not possible to speak of God 'as he is in himself', and this is true if it means that God as he is in himself is someone different from him who is disclosed to faith in Jesus, from him who confronts us in this world. There is no other God. But it is not true if, through whatever worthy motive of stopping speculations of the 'alien God' variety, it means that our descriptions of God must be limited to timid generalizations of mystery or otherness or beyondness. If our descriptions are so limited, then they can amount to very little of any importance, certainly not enough to convince us of what ultimately matters, what is really real. In fact, however, even the proponents of 'historical transcendence' do say more than this: they say that the only being of God is his being-for-others, which may even be analysed as a circumlocution for the traditional word 'love'.[8]

4 We in our turn have no hesitation in speaking about God 'as he is in himself', and we shall do this not through the analysis of any concept like 'person' or 'otherness' or 'transcendence', but on the basis of our faith that Jesus in his acting and action, in the whole context of his history, has given us the entrée, as it were, or the right perspective, to enable us to speak truly of God.

4.1 This does not mean that we are abandoning the 'otherness' of God. We could not do that without distorting all the data for our language about him. We cannot comprehend him in the sense of encompassing him in our own concepts and systems of thought. But we can apprehend him, and what we apprehend is no more a giant question mark than a giant man. In thinking about this, it may be that the concept of transcendence, whether metaphysical or historical, creates more trouble than it solves. 'Transcending', after all, is a transitive verb, it must have an object. On its own, it is not an activity to which we can assign any recognizable meaning. 'The balloon ascends' is meaningful; so is 'the elevator descends'. But 'the balloon transcends' and 'the elevator transcends' and 'I transcend' and 'Smith transcends' are all meaningless. On the face of it, 'God transcends' is also nonsense. 'Transcendence', then, cannot of itself refer to an activity of things or men or God.

4.2 It is, rather, a relational term. It indicates something about the relation between one thing and another. 'God's goodness transcends human goodness' is a way of saying that the former is related to, but not limited to, the latter. So with his justice, his knowledge, his power, above all his love. 'Related to' but 'not limited by'. Whenever we use the word transcendent, we have in mind two sides of a relation. Sheer transcendence, like sheer otherness, is as much a linguistic impossibility as a philosophical one. Nothing but confusion can be looked for if this is forgotten. An equally serious result ensues if, in a fit of zeal for systematizing, the attempt is made to lump together all the ways in which God transcends human experience and limitations so as to end up with a composite notion of 'transcendence'. It can mean nothing until it is unpackaged again and the various elements it contains examined separately. Instead, therefore, of giving a straight endorsement of the contention that God's transcendence is to be understood historically rather than metaphysically, we should do better to try to summarize the various ideas that this notion of transcendence is intended to convey, bearing in mind the question with which we started, 'Where is God?'

5.1 When we say that God transcends this world, we are acknowledging that he is not to be identified with it. He is other than it or the people in it. This is not to say that he 'inhabits' some non-physical 'space' that we might identify or claim to know anything about (metaphysical transcendence). But it does mean that we can never with our human language and concepts say all there is to be said about him.

5.2 But we must immediately go on to affirm that even though he is 'other' in that sense, he is not alien to the world or to us. One might almost say that this is what the Christian gospel is all about. If it were to be summed up in one word it would be the Hebrew word *Immanuel*, which literally means 'God with us'. Though he is other, he is related to every one of us and every thing in our universe: he cares for us, he is concerned for all. But this is to anticipate, and we shall return to this when we investigate what is meant by the love of God. For the moment, it is enough to insist that while he transcends the finite existence which is the only existence we can know, he is related to it. It is his in so far as it is his concern. Indeed, it would be true to say that he can only transcend it because he is related to it.

5.3 At various times and in various places, some expressions have struck a chord with men as being particularly appropriate to indicate this relationship. At one time, the otherness of God seemed so predominant that it was necessary to think of him as being high above, exalted, beyond this world. At other times, 'with-us-ness' has assumed the dominant role, so that the total emphasis was placed on the identification of God in the world, in us. Or again, God has at times been envisaged as circling the universe, upholding its processes and regularities but not 'interfering' with what went on in it. Yet again, the mystery and profundity of this relationship seems best described in terms of depth: God is to be found in the depth of our being, as the ground of our being. Perhaps, today, we can best envisage God as ahead of us, awaiting us in the open future that lies before us, beckoning us on, as it were, with our fellow men, not out of fear, or magic, or determined power, but out of love.

5.4 In all these ways – up, within, around, down, ahead – has the relation with God been described. But though one way may at one time have been more prominent in men's minds than another, the Christian view of God as reality has at all times been a complex of all these ways. The astonishing thing about the language of the Bible is, as has been indicated, that even though its authors shared a primitive picture of the universe which allowed for what we would call a physical heaven, they found it necessary, in their response to reality, to speak of God in all these ways without committing themselves exclusively to any one. 'If I ascend up into heaven, Thou art there' (Ps. 139.8: height); 'The word is very nigh unto thee, in thy mouth and in thy heart that thou mayest do it' (Deut. 30.14: immanence); 'Before the mountains were brought forth or ever Thou hadst formed the earth and the world, even from everlasting to everlasting Thou art God' (Ps. 90.2: priority); 'Thou hast beset me behind and before' (Ps. 139.5: encircling); 'If I make my bed in hell, behold Thou art there' (Ps. 139.8: depth); 'Thou preparest a place before me in the presence of mine enemies' (Ps. 23.5): the promised land theme, the promised Sabbath rest (God in the future). These illustrations should suffice to show the astonishing wealth of imagery which the biblical writers felt constrained to use as they tried to acknowledge that God is both in every nook and cranny of our physical world and experience and yet beyond it, not confined to it.

6 Where, then, is God? Negatively, we can only answer that he is not restricted to the confines of our physical universe or our present experience. We cannot speculate further. Positively, it seems as if our data would compel us to say that he is here, there and everywhere, and this is indeed what the Christian perspective is. But the uniqueness of the Christian perspective is this: that God is to be known here there and everywhere because he is definitively known in one place – in Jesus Christ. Because he is to be known forever there, he is to be known everywhere, in the darkest corners and moments as well as the brightest, in failure and success, in the present and the future, in life and even in death. How can these things be? There is no need to fall back on an answer of total mystery. We can go further, and try now to understand what is meant by the strange claim that God is love.

NOTES

1. Dietrich Bonhoeffer, *Letters and Papers from Prison*, Revised Edition (London: SCM Press; New York: The Macmillan Company, 1967), p. 210.

2. R. Gregor Smith, *Secular Christianity* (London: Collins; New York: Harper and Row, 1966), p. 122.

3. Martin Buber, *I and Thou* (Edinburgh: T. and T. Clark, 1937), p. 6.

4. R. Gregor Smith, *op. cit.*, p. 122.

5. R. Gregor Smith, *op. cit.*, p. 124.

6. R. Gregor Smith, *op. cit.*, p. 123.

7. Joseph Haroutunian, *God with Us* (Philadelphia: Westminster Press; London: Epworth Press, 1967).

8. R. Gregor Smith, *op. cit.*, p. 124.

5 'Love is the Greatest Thing'

1 Several references have already been made to the love of God. When we were talking about how God is known, we mentioned that it is the fact that he is love that makes a total personal response the only appropriate means of knowledge of him. When we were looking at how he transcends our world and experience, we referred to a modern description of his being as 'being for others – a circumlocution for love'. Now we must examine what Christians mean when they speak about the love of God, or God as love.

1.1 It had better be acknowledged at the outset that this is no simple task, for there are weighty reasons for avoiding this word 'love' altogether in this context. For one thing, in our age it has associations of sheer sentimentality. The love story of the women's magazine, the love ballad (euphemistically so-called) of the 'pop scene', the love epic of the screen – these are all so overloaded with sloppiness, so unrelated to the mundane and realistic facts of the world we actually live in as to suggest an embargo on the word 'love' as a serious description of what is real.

1.2 Less generally, the history of theology provides warnings that where emphasis is placed in an unspecified way on the love of God, the gospel can easily be turned into a naïve belief in inevitable progress on the one hand, or a complacent affirmation that 'God will provide', on the other. In either case, the consequence can be a refusal to be realistic about the more unpleasant facts of existence, with the corollary that resistance to evil, social or personal, is undermined.

1.3 A word, then, which is so overloaded with popular

associations of this type would seem on the face of it to have forfeited all possibility of communicating what is ultimately real, who God is. The obstacle is not so much the sexual connotation. Thanks largely to the researches of psychologists, Christian thinkers have been forced to re-examine what was thought to be traditional teaching on sex as something base, and animal, part of our 'lower nature', something which had to be endured, if it could not be denied without leading to something worse. They now see that it has a much more positive role in human life, that it can and must be integrated constructively with every other human instinct and aspiration if life as a whole is to be a total response to reality. The obstacle which the popular associations of 'love' provide to speaking of God as love is rather that they are almost exclusively emotional. If love is an emotion, and if emotions are as fickle as (with good reason) we have been led to believe they are, what stability, or certainty or hope is to be provided by a god who is an emotion?

1.4 There is another difficulty of speaking of God as love, and that is it can easily appear callous, even cruel. The difficulties we have already mentioned – sentimentality, arbitrary emotionalism – are real enough in the context of the well-fed members of the Western world. In the wider context which includes the majority of the earth's inhabitants, to speak of ultimate reality as love could appear as irony carried to satanic extremes. In the context of the developing countries of our planet, what right has anyone to speak of love when what is wanted is only a little more of life? What point is there in speaking of the problem of meaning, when the real problem is the problem of survival? No amount of sincerity, or piety for that matter, can disguise the fact that the man with a well-stocked larder who tells a starving crowd, 'Man does not live by bread alone', is a hypocrite, and for that reason cannot and should not be taken seriously. Similarly, proclaiming a message of love in circumstances which speak much more eloquently of misery, deprivation, neglect and indifference, with death as a possible escape from meaninglessness – that is a dangerous enterprise.

2   Formidable as these difficulties are, they can only serve notice on us to proceed with caution. They cannot be allowed to bring us to a halt. For all our data for reality – the story which scripture has to tell, the historical experience of the Church, even our own experience of what is real in our personal life with other persons – impel us to try to speak of God realistically in terms of love. We have already pointed out that the biblical writers did not go in for abstract philosophizing about the nature of God. But, occasionally, there are one-sentence summaries which take us to the very heart and secret of the Gospel. St John in his gospel offers one such summary with his famous saying, 'God loved the world so much that he gave his only Son, that everyone who has faith in him may not die but have eternal life' (John 3.16). Even more briefly, he sums up the whole witness of the Old Testament, the New Testament, the life of the Church in all ages, in these words, 'God is love' (1 John 4.8).

3   If we say that 'God is love' is the whole of the gospel, the last word on who God is, we must be careful to stress that it is the gospel of God as love that is meant; not the gospel of love in general or some particular idea of love. Perhaps this is too obvious to need stating. But it is surprising how easily it can be turned into something quite different. Having extracted from the gospel the idea that 'God is love', it is all too easy – indeed it has happened so frequently in the history of Christian thought as to appear almost natural – for us to leave the original context far behind and to reverse the terms so that the emphasis is totally misplaced. Not 'God is love', now, but 'love is God'. When that happens, the idea of love loses its anchorage in the gospel and drifts into a sea of personal preferences. 'Love' now stands for what an individual or group happens to find congenial or to think that it needs, and underneath the unity which the common use of this word suggests there will lurk an anarchy of differing, even contradictory desires. We have seen a striking example of this in recent years in the

'Hippie' or 'Flower Power' movement which in its heyday reached remarkable proportions among the young in the U.S.A. and to a lesser extent in Europe. These young people experienced a common revulsion against the values of a rigidly materialistic society and were courageous enough to seek something better. What they wanted was to dedicate their lives to 'love' as the ultimate reality, as God for them. But it all proved to be a passing, even if moving and highly colourful phenomenon. Their ultimate reality proved to be an illusion. Their God was their own idea of love, not the God who is love, of the Christian gospel.

The fate of the Hippies should help us to see how we must proceed if we are to explain the meaning of love in the sentence 'God is love'. In effect, the most satisfactory commentary would be a repetition in our own words of the biblical story. This means that we have to try to understand the love of God in terms of what happens, rather than by an analysis of certain components, in terms of what God 'does' rather than in terms of what he 'consists of'.

3.1 Christians believe that this can only be done by allowing Jesus of Nazareth to put content into what is meant by love when we say God is love. It is important to realize that it is not here simply a question of what Jesus taught about the love of God. He did, of course, teach much and his teaching often seemed highly original and revolutionary in its implications. Not without cause has he been called 'mankind's teacher'. But it is not simply that he is mankind's teacher. The Christian belief is that in Jesus, God himself is active, giving himself totally and without reserve. It would be entirely in accord with their – and the New Testament's – way of looking at things if we were to think of Jesus as mankind's lover. For the astonishing claim which Christians dare to make is that Jesus is God's love in action. For this reason, it is what he does as much as what he says and teaches which puts content for us into the love of God.

3.2 It is not being suggested that we isolate Jesus from the context in which he is proclaimed as Christ, as the

Anointed One. We have no data for understanding him otherwise than as a Jew, whose sole source of knowledge of God was Jewish worship and the witness of the Old Testament. The only Jesus we know anything about is he whom his disciples proclaimed as the Messiah. So in attempting to allow Jesus to put content into our notion of the love of God, we may not forsake the Old Testament scripture for an alleged concentration on the New.

4 In our consideration of God as love, then, we do not start with a claim to know what love is and then attribute it to God in a supreme degree. Rather, we shall allow our data to tell us what love is. Instead of having one simple meaning, we shall find it a highly complex affair to be treated, as it has been well put, as a 'constellation of meaning'.[1] All we can attempt here is to indicate in modern terminology the principal features of the main points or 'stars' in this constellation, giving some account of their relation to one another and to other parts of reality.

4.1 Let us start, then, and consider a first point in our constellation, the element of *concern* in the love of God. This is an ordinary enough word, some may say too ordinary for such an exalted theme. But at least we know what is ordinarily meant when we talk of human concern and it is generally agreed that it is a feature of love between humans. At a human level, to be concerned about someone is to care, and not only for that person in himself but in his relation with other people, things and circumstances. It is not only a matter of seeking his welfare, of our will to do him well: it is also a matter of our getting to know him better, of our feelings for him. It is not by accident that in certain settings 'to be anxious about someone' is synonymous with concern. Furthermore, if I am concerned about someone, I have, by this very fact, invested him with value. He matters – at least to me.

If we turn now from concern as an element in human love, to concern in God, we find that it has much in common with human concern, though there are important differences.

4.1.1 That God knows and understands the lot, the

predicament of his creatures is the constant witness of the Bible and experience of the Church. 'He knoweth our frame; He remembereth we are dust' (Ps. 103.14), cried the Psalmist; and again, 'Thou knowest my downsitting and mine uprising, Thou understandest my thought afar off' (Ps. 139.2); 'Do not ask anxiously, "What are we to eat? What are we to drink? What shall we wear?"', said Jesus, and gave the reason: 'Your heavenly Father knows that you need them all' (Matt. 6.31 f.). St Paul, too, expressed his confidence in God's understanding and knowing what we required before we even prayed (Rom. 8.26 f.), and looked forward to a time when 'I shall know, even as I am known' (1 Cor. 13.12). But how does God know? The traditional answer is that he knows because he has 'made' us, he knows us as our Creator. As in sculpture, no one knows his creation better than the sculptor; as in pottery, if anyone knows the pot it is the potter (cf. Jer. 18.1–10). But this way of looking at the divine knowledge is not without its difficulties. Human beings may live pretty dull lives, but they are not pots. More important, this approach restricts knowledge to what might be called external knowledge, knowledge from without. But the best kind of knowledge we can envisage is 'inside' knowledge, knowledge of a situation from within. For this, more is required than mere book learning or the assembly and correlation of all the relevant facts. The additional factor for 'inside' knowledge is knowing what it is like from the inside, from within the situation. Now this is precisely what Christians believe to be involved in Incarnation, in God's being with men as a man, Jesus. That is how God's love expresses itself as concern – in a life lived. That, too, is the basis of our conviction that God understands us and everything that is: not simply because he has set up a relation of creator to creature (the potter-pot image), but rather because he has chosen us as the object of his concern.

4.1.2 God's concern, then, is a knowing concern. Another way of putting this, important enough, however, to be considered in its own right, is to say that God's concern is a sensitive concern. Some people are clearly more sensitive than others. One man, with the best will in the world, can go bursting into a room where two others have just had an almighty row and, being entirely ignorant of the situation, proceed with one remark to start up the altercation all over again. Another man in the same circumstances will somehow sense that all is not well, he will be sensitive to the 'atmosphere' and act accordingly. Sensitivity does yield a kind of knowledge, and an important kind of knowledge at that.

For God, we claim that his 'inside knowledge' of us is so complete, that he is so sensitive to our needs and to our way of behaving that he knows what we have done, what we are thinking, feeling and hoping and what we will do. In this sense, his knowledge is infinite: no detail of our existence is unappreciated or unforeseen by him.

It has always been the Christian claim that God's knowledge of the future is as complete as his knowledge of the present and the past. To many people, this has been taken to imply that every detail of our existence has been planned in advance, determined, pre-planned in computer fashion. This implication in its turn has seemed to pose a permanent question-mark against anything worthy of the name of human freedom. If everything is determined beforehand, without our co-operation, then our choices, our resolutions, our commitments can in no sense be free (nor, incidentally, could we be in any meaningful sense responsible for them). But this conclusion, unhealthy as it is unrealistic, does not follow if we refuse to think of God's knowledge as a mechanical super-power. If, on the contrary, we think of it primarily as knowledge born of hyper-sensitivity, as a reflection of his concern, then it is meaningful to insist both that he knows everything that is and will be and that we have a measure of freedom to do what we choose to do (including the freedom to make and be responsible for our own mistakes). To pursue the computer analogy a little further, it is not unhelpful to think of God's store of knowledge as a giant self-programming computer.[2] Only we must go on to say that the data stored in the computer has not been gathered mechanically or automatically or as a matter of course. It is the product of the divine sensitivity exercised in concern.

4.1.3 Sensitivity in action becomes, literally, compassion, and it is therefore not surprising that the compassion of God should be one of the greatest of biblical themes. In passage after passage in the Old Testament, witness is borne to faith in God who enters into the predicaments of his people, but supremely in the New Testament, sensitivity in action is presented as a living man. Jesus suffers as much with others as he suffers for them, and in his suffering Christians find the ultimate expression of the compassion of God. Indeed, it is this compassionate concern of God which alone imparts value and infinite worth to human life and human lives.

4.2 The theme of concern as an aspect of the love of God is not forsaken if we direct attention to the next point in the constellation already referred to. For by looking at our data from the perspective of concern, another major motif can be discerned. That is love as *commitment*.

It would be no novelty to point to the importance of commitment in all facets of living. Commitment to one's subject as the necessary condition for advance in knowledge, scientific as much as artistic; the businessman's commitment to his product, as much as the poet's commitment to his vision; commitment to another as the presupposition of personal knowledge; in many different ways, the key role of commitment is now widely recognized. Especially in theology, both the impossibility of an 'uncommitted' knowledge of God and the necessity of commitment for faith are admitted. But what must now be maintained is not so much the importance of commitment in human response to God as its prominence in God's relation to his creation, as a feature of his love. For it can hold together, uniting, as it were, under the banner of love, a number of indispensable elements of our data.

4.2.1 Commitment includes, for example, the ideas of choice or decision, and pledging and promise which loom so large in the biblical witness to God. Israel is presented above all as a 'covenanted people', chosen, elected by Yahweh among all the nations of earth for his own purpose, which is a special purpose not just for the sake of Israel but for the sake of all peoples. This notion of covenant between God and man is undoubtedly a difficult one for our age to grasp. We are too literal-minded: we find some of the highly picturesque references in the Old Testament to God's making a bargain with individuals and groups bewildering, if not offensive, and tend to dismiss them as too primitive, too crude. But if we read what the Bible has to say about 'covenant' rather as an expression of Israel's conviction of God's commitment to mankind, working itself out in the history of a people and reaching a climax in the man Jesus, living his commitment to the world, then it becomes possible to re-examine the notion of covenant with a new seriousness and urgency. 'He entered his own realm', and though 'his own would not receive him' (John 1.11) yet he kept them safe to the last, so that the truth of Jesus' statement to his disciples remains an abiding expression of Christian experience: 'you did not choose me: I chose you' (John 15.16).

4.2.2 In a similar way, the allied notion of the faithfulness of God can be seen without difficulty in the light of his commitment. In Israel's experience, God's inexplicable faithfulness is such that he is to be relied on, totally, even when lack of obedience and concern on the part of Israel would, by any human standard, justify rejection. Yet even when God is rejected, ignored, despised – and here Christians' minds inevitably turn to Golgotha and Calvary – even then God keeps faith, with infinite patience, perseverance and longsuffering. In Jesus' faithfulness 'unto death', Christians see the last word in what the faithfulness of God means, what kind of commitment is here at stake, what sort of love is the love of God. In the Hebrew language there is the most intimate connection between faithfulness and truth, and both are held together by the word 'Amen'. This was not in Hebrew what it has so often become in Christendom, a conventional and convenient way of bringing a prayer or a hymn to an end. It indicated rather, 'this is the truth' because 'this can be relied on', and the reason anything could be relied on was because it was founded on the faithfulness not of abstract reasoning, but of God. That God was and is true to his word, to his commitment, is indeed the great Amen. But it is more than that; through commitment it can be seen as an expression of love.

4.3 This glimpse of commitment in action makes it necessary to consider *communication* as yet one more aspect of the love of God.

At first sight, 'communication' is an unlikely candidate for inclusion in this context. It seems too neutral, too bloodless a term to keep company with 'concern' and 'commitment'. It speaks of roads and railways, of envelopes and telephone wires, of radios and satellites. But these things are not communication, they merely provide the opportunity. Communication is what happens between people, when something is said or sent or given, and received for what it is. Failure in communication is what happens when one person (or class, or nation, or race) cannot get through to another, and it requires no gift of prophecy to see that multi-dimensional breakdown in communication is at the back of the mid-twentieth century malaise. What we are now saying is that just as between human beings there can be no love without communication, so with God, communication is a definitive element in love. Commitment without communication must forever remain frustrated, unfulfilled, theoretical only.

4.3.1 How does the data for our knowledge of God entitle us to speak of love as communication? The obvious presupposition of Israelite religion is that God does communicate with his people – and this in a variety of ways. 'Thus saith the Lord' was the constant refrain of the prophets, as they interpreted the events of their times in the light of reality as it had been given to them to know. The great Exodus experience was interpreted above all as God's work, his having brought them up, across the Red Sea, out of the land of Egypt, thereby committing himself to them in history. In the same way, the Law by which they lived and the cult by which they worshipped were no man-made devices. They were seen as the means by which God himself provided for the appropriate response of his people to him, to further the fulfilment of his purpose for creation. His will for the present (to be responded to in obedient living) and for the future (establishing a living hope) were thus communicated.

4.3.2 In the New Testament, however, the events centred on Jesus of Nazareth are not interpreted merely as a more precise declaration of the will of God. Now St John, for example, can speak of the 'Word' becoming 'flesh' (John 1.14) in a life real and in no sense illusory. God's Word is now no longer spoken (by the mouth of a prophet or otherwise): it is a historical reality, a life lived, Jesus. He is proclaimed by his disciples after his death not merely as the One through whom God communicates, the greatest teacher. He is God's communication of himself. As God's self-communication, Jesus is God's full and final word to mankind. If he gives himself, and not just hints or even truths about himself, what more is there to give?

4.3.3 This self-communication of God, of reality, is such, so personal, we might say, that it can never be turned into a general truth, which might be discerned or debated in theory or in the abstract. It is a precise communication which can only be received by the total life reaction of the person to whom it is addressed (and it is addressed to all). It is self-authenticating, which is another way of saying that there are no external guarantees, such as thunder or lightning or sacred formulae or even a soft, warm glow in the heart. This means that we must still speak in terms of 'mystery', with no simple or easy identification. But the communication which is an essential feature of God's love is not illusory: the response to it will serve the very purpose and bear the very marks of divine love.

4.4 Having seen that the element of communication in God's love is such that it does not stop short of complete self-giving, we have in fact arrived at the deepest level of our exploration. For now we can consider God's love as *identification*.

4.4.1 In human affairs, the mere fact of involvement is no guarantee of love. It could, on the contrary, point merely to self-gratification. This is the case with the dilettante, 'playing' at art, for example. It is also the case with the 'do-gooder', who is quite prepared to get involved in good causes, even in the problems and predicaments of others, provided that there is no real question of the would-be benefactor compromising himself, being misunderstood or getting hurt. But once the degree of involvement reaches the stage at which one person is actually identifying with another, then the point of no return has been passed, there is no more insulation against risk or hurt or harm; and it becomes appropriate to speak of love.

Love as identification – that is what Christians mean by the doctrine of Incarnation, the Word made flesh, God made man in Jesus Christ. This is neither a primitive nor a sophisticated way of expressing an idea or a hope. It is the declaration of something that has happened, creating a new state of affairs, rich with new possibilities. For Incarnation means that God has involved himself totally, without reserve, in the historical actualities, the rough and tumble, the conditions, hopes and fears of human life.

4.4.2 For this reason it is necessary to take with absolute seriousness the real historical involvement of Jesus as a real person among real people. There can be no bypassing this or taking it lightly, despite all the attendant disadvantages, despite possible misunderstandings, despite inevitable misinterpretations of his words and his actions. During his life he was wilfully misunderstood by the religious authorities, the ordinary people misinterpreted him, even his disciples did not wholly understand him; and after his death, even their acknowledgment of his risen presence with them has not prevented his followers time and again falsifying his history and misapplying the scriptural witness to him. But these are the risks that love takes. They could only have been avoided if the Incarnation had been less than total and identification less than complete.

4.4.3 It is, however, necessary to go further. For in

Jesus, Christians claim to know God identifying himself not merely with suffering humanity but actually with sinful humanity. Because there is no reservation or qualification of this identification, it is not enough to see the life and ministry and death of Jesus as pointing to some reality beyond. Because it is love identifying itself with sinful humanity, we can see the Cross not as pointing to something beyond but as the fact of God's willingness and ability to take himself and so forgive the sins of men.

In Christian doctrine, teaching on the divine forgiveness of sins and reconciliation of men to God is known as the doctrine of Atonement, and in the history of Christian thought, many strange theories have been propounded to describe and account for the forgiveness which the Gospel proclaims and the Church attests. But to see love as identification is to have the key to understanding forgiveness. Sin is not forgotten, or played down, or treated as something less serious than it actually is. But when God identifies with the sinner it is accepted and expressed in all its seriousness, with all its consequences and all its risks. Only love of a supreme kind can take such a risk and emerge triumphant. Only perfect love can dare to risk losing itself in such an act of total identification for the sake of forgiveness, reconciliation and peace. The Christian claim is not that Jesus of Nazareth illustrates this love, or teaches it, or points to it. It is rather that he is this love in ultimate action.

4.4.4 Reference has been made to such identifying love emerging triumphant and taking the risk of losing itself. This would seem to invite the comment, Has it in fact emerged triumphant, has it in fact not lost itself? This is fair comment. It is perfectly true that identification is a final stage, a final commitment. If it is total and real and not just partial and apparent, there can be no unscrambling, no 'de-identification' which would not prove that it was not identification proper in the first place. This being so, could it not be that when Jesus breathed his last breath – and no one could now argue that his death was not a real physical death – perfect love reached its end? This possibility cannot

95

be dismissed, however preposterous or offensive it might to some appear. For it was a possibility. Such is the risk which perfect love takes. But that this possibility was not actualized is the message of Easter which Christians accept as their own.

'On the third day he rose again.' Christian faith is Resurrection faith, and it is important to realize that everything that was written of Jesus, everything that was told about him was told from a post-Easter situation. It is only because of Easter that we know anything about Jesus at all. 'What actually happened' that first Easter, we shall never know, if by 'know' we mean some sort of neutral, allegedly objective account either of the mechanics of resurrection or how we in the twentieth century would have described what the disciples saw, or what a candid camera might or might not have revealed. But what we do maintain and have good grounds for maintaining is that the cry of astonishment, 'Jesus lives!', was no illusion. Jesus was in some way personally present to his disciples, giving them the conviction that his death was not the end of the story but the beginning, the beginning of a new understanding of reality, new possibilities of life. Christian faith is Resurrection faith not because Christians in all ages accept, at second-hand, that the earliest disciples were telling the truth. It is Resurrection faith because twentieth century Christians can share the same conviction, the same understanding as that of those first Easter Christians, that literally nothing is able, now or hereafter, to come between them and 'the love of God in Christ Jesus' (Rom. 8.39).

4.5 Having reached the point of describing God's love as identification, we have arrived at the deepest level of love: it is not possible to go further than that. Identifying love is the very essence of God. In this brief outline, we have not, of course, exhausted all that there is to be said on this subject. We may, however, usefully conclude the survey by indicating something of the consequences which flow from this love, thereby putting more precise content into its meaning. If the love of God is to be treated dynamically, as has been maintained, instead of statically, it is appropriate to take account of the situation it creates and the response it evokes.

5.1 From this point of view, the love of God is a reconciling love: it makes itself known as community. One of the most dangerous distortions of the Gospel is excessive individualism, which sees the end-product of God's love as a rescue operation for isolated individuals, plucking them out from among their fellows and their environment to give them some sort of status of superiority and immunity. This is a distortion because it fails to appreciate either the immense range of God's love or the totality of his identification in Jesus Christ. But it is also a distortion because it fails to take account of the Christian claim that by his act of identification, God has both given himself to mankind and opened man's eyes to each other, even to 'the least of these my brethren' (Matt. 25.40). By his act of reconciliation, he has reconciled men to each other. 'God was in Christ reconciling the world to himself, no longer holding men's misdeeds against them', and, the Apostle Paul continues, 'has entrusted us with the message of reconciliation' (II Cor. 5.19). Other New Testament passages are just as explicit: 'Gentile and Jews, he has made the two one, and in his own body of flesh and blood has broken down the enmity which stood like a dividing wall between them' (Eph. 2.13 f.). 'There is no such thing as Jew and Greek, slave and freeman, male and female; for you are all one person in Christ Jesus' (Gal. 3.28).

This is not to be understood as an exalted, high-pitched way of making the rather simple point that we are 'all Jock Tamson's bairns', that as members of the same species we are in the same soup together and share the same fate. Nor does it deny that men are in fact cruelly divided, that they still hate and fear and want to and do kill each other. But it does mean that there is an underlying unity of men, a unity constituted by love, God's love. It was no sentimental dreamer, but a man steeped in the social and political problems of his time who said somewhere: 'Love binds

D

society from within, it is both lynch-pin and girdle, and it can never be annihilated.[3]

5.2.1 It is a short step from recognizing love as community to seeing that it is of the essence of God's love to beget love. For sharing in God's love is the only legitimate response to it. There can be no knowledge of God without it. One of the New Testament writers can be uncomfortably blunt about this: 'The unloving know nothing of God' (I John 4.8); 'If a man says, "I love God" while hating his brother, he is a liar' (I John 4.20). Certainly, there can be no question of talking ourselves into loving our neighbours, or forcing ourselves or anyone else to do so. That can only lead to self-deception, disintegration and even psychological breakdown. We are not to love our neighbour in order to know God and love him; but because he loves us, it becomes possible and necessary. The situation seems to be that the final manifestation and triumph of his love in Jesus Christ puts us in a new situation, setting us within a whole new network of relationships each with a whole new range of possibilities.

5.2.2 The universal range of God's love and the corresponding complexity of the network of relations which it creates, means that the expression of love in these relations can assume widely differing forms. It must be said that the Church is only beginning to recognize just how many and how different the appropriate forms of love can be. For too long, 'Love thy neighbour' has been interpreted in a highly individual sense, from 'be nice to people' at one end of the scale, to 'do as many good turns as possible for individuals you come across', at the other. This individualistic interpretation, backed as it usually was by a private ethic the main feature of which was the resolve to keep oneself uncontaminated by the evils of the world, enabled men to live out their lives in unquestioning acquiescence in impersonal systems of economic exploitation and political oppression which were a total denial of love.

But we see now that the love which is a response to God's love cannot be restricted to kindly acts accompanied by benevolent feelings for single individuals. It extends to groups beyond the range of our immediate acquaintance, to nations and races with whom it is impossible for us to have any personal contact at all, to likeminded and very different minded, from our friend next door to millions on the other side of the world who may even be our legal enemies. In this situation the appropriate form for the expression of love will be infinitely variable, and often very unromantic. Sometimes, where personal knowledge is out of the question, it will take the form of a simple demand for justice, love at long range, as it were. Sometimes, it will be a question of gathering information, for a realistic account of the situation, of what is going on, is the necessary condition of realistic action. In this sense, probing the mysteries of economic or social systems, or mastering the details of technology, or investigating the mechanics of aid and trade with other countries, can be genuine acts of love. Sometimes it can take dangerous and unpleasant forms. In some situations the only way of realistically expressing love for the oppressed may be identification and engagement in revolution, with all the unloving possibilities that the word implies. Sometimes, it may be something quite ordinary and mundane, like doing the job one's paid for, faithfully and well. In short, there is no end to the variety of forms love can take.

5.3.1 Finally, God's love is a liberating love. It frees for love. Indeed, if the appropriate response to love is love, then it must follow that this response is free, for love is the one thing that cannot be forced: if it is not free, it is not love. On reflection, therefore, it is not surprising that freedom is a constantly recurring theme of the New Testament. 'You shall know the truth, and the truth will set you free' (John 8.32), is the promise. 'You are therefore no longer a slave but a son' (Gal. 4.7). 'Christ set us free, to be free men' (Gal. 5.1) is the declaration of the present state of affairs. In New Testament terms, the freedom made available is solidly grounded in who Jesus was and what he has done. Further, when the whole life of Jesus as presented in the Gospels – what he said and did, with whom and to whom –

is looked at from the perspective of freedom, it is easy to understand why many commentators have found there the normative expression of freedom in human life. Here is total freedom for others without restriction, for all sorts, in all conditions, in all circumstances. Indeed, so striking is this freedom that one recent author can make out a good case for understanding the Gospel as the good news of the free man Jesus whose freedom, after his death, became and becomes 'contagious' among his disciples.[4] And certainly, there is no lack of disciples ancient or modern who have willingly testified that in giving their personal backing to love as the ultimate reality, to God's love, they have both discovered themselves for the first time and known themselves to be free.

5.3.2 Just as we had to show that the love begotten of God's love was nothing sloppy, sentimental or make-believe, so now it has to be stated in plain terms that the freedom of love is no unrestrained orgy of pursuing the fancy of the moment. This is not easy to do without hypocrisy in the society of the Western world, where so many pressures are at work to persuade us to get and gain in order to spend and enjoy. In traditional (though unpopular) terms, it must be re-affirmed that such is not freedom but tyranny of the emotions, and the fact of having money enough to give full rein to such tyranny merely confirms it. There is no loneliness like the loneliness of the millionaire. So, too, before extolling the freedom of the Gospel, the freedom of love, it is necessary to accept realistically everything that the medical and social sciences have to teach of the factors which affect, if not determine, human behaviour: an individual's physical and psychological make-up, environmental influences, the kind of people his parents were, the whole complex of social, economic, even geographical circumstances, which contribute towards making a man what he is. Nothing but harm can come from failure to reckon with this fast-growing body of knowledge and insight into why people do the things they do. For the Christian claim is not that God's gift of love removes us from the sphere of operation of all these influences, nor is it that in that sphere, Christians are, as if by magic, immunized against their harmful effects. The Christian claim is that in that very sphere God as love is present, accepting and reconciling in that very place, offering himself as ultimate reality to be accepted or rejected, enabling those who accept to accept themselves to the point of being able to laugh at themselves, and, freed as they are for others, to make a convinced and consistent reponse.

NOTES

1. See John McIntyre, *On the Love of God* (Collins, 1962), to which I am largely indebted for what follows.

2. For this illustration see the preceding volume in this series: John Hick, *Christianity at the Centre* (London: SCM Press, 1968), pp. 24 ff.

3. Kagawa of Japan.

4. Paul van Buren, *The Secular Meaning of the Gospel* (London: SCM Press; New York: The Macmillan Company, 1963).

6   All this 'Omni-' Business

1   In the last chapter, we tried to indicate what the sentence 'God is love' means. We treated this sentence not so much as a definition of God as a summing-up of the most important things that can be said of God on the basis of the biblical claims and of the Church's and the individual Christian's experienced response to them. This meant that we could not speak of God's love statically, as some quality or attribute or thing (among other qualities, attributes or things) which God has. We had to speak of it dynamically, as what God is, specifically in terms of a life lived, Jesus Christ, and so speak not only of qualities but of actions, attitudes, responses and new situations created. In a word, we tried to let Jesus Christ, seen against the background of the Old Testament, proclaimed in the New, worshipped in the Church, identifying with all other people, put content into this word 'love'. In this way, we sought to avoid both abstract speculation and unbridled wishful thinking, while yet insisting that we do know what we are talking about when we talk of God as love and see this as the heart of the Gospel, the essential thing that can and must be said of him.

1.1   Now, however, we have to face the consequences of this total emphasis on God as love. In doing so, we can anticipate complaints, from many quarters, to the effect that this is all too one-sided a presentation. Does it not ignore or even deny too many of those aspects of God which Christians have always believed in or at least claimed to believe in? Perhaps less congenial, more frightening aspects, like the divine righteousness, even wrath? Or less intelligible aspects, like the 'omnipotence', 'omniscience', 'omnipresence', 'omnivolence' of God, aspects which, in spite of all the difficulties, have been held on to in one way or another in Christian teaching throughout the centuries? Or aspects of mystery, such as majesty and holiness and glory, so important for worship and which have served so well in preserving a proper humility in human speech about God? Do all these now just disappear, once we understand God as love?

1.2 Let it be admitted that such a disappearance would not be altogether unpopular. There are those who see any ideas of the righteousness or wrath of God as functioning only to create and stimulate destructive and illusory feelings of guilt. Again, there are those who find such notions as 'omnipotence' intellectually indefensible. In the words of one avant-garde Christian: 'All this omni-business is mere overbelief . . . extrapolating to the skies'.[1] Or again, not a few would be glad to see a soft-pedalling of the aspects of mystery; in a world 'come of age' and fully responsible for its own actions, emphasis on mystery can only lead to a world-denying mysticism which relativizes any human aspiration and takes the steam out of serious attempts to 'love one's neighbour'.

2 Our answer to both the complainants and the welcomers is that such aspects cannot be allowed to disappear. Quite simply, a faithful interpretation of the data will not permit it. Those traditional aspects were not just dreamed up by chance. They emerged and were ratified only after profound and constant reflection on reality as it presented itself. To allow such disappearance would be to do violence to the biblical evidence and to the evidence of individual and collective experience. On the other hand, there can be no going back on what we believe of God as love. This means that all these other aspects cannot share pride of place with 'love' in our understanding of God. It would be morally intolerable and intellectually indefensible if we were to arrive at a vision of God who was now forgiving, now 'justly punishing'; now knowable, now unknowable; now 'saving', now leaving men to 'their just reward'. All these other

103

aspects, then, if they are to be retained – and our contention is that they must be retained – have to be understood in the light of God's love. They have a place, an essential place, but they do not have pride of place. The aim of this chapter, then, is to shew how some of these traditional aspects may help to illumine our understanding of God, but only as they are interpreted in the light of his love.

2.1 Let us begin with the righteousness of God. The picture of God as the just judge who can neither do nor tolerate wrong is a familiar one. According to this picture, he is in a position to pass judgment on what goes on in the world, and, looking down from his heavenly bench, he finds all men falling short of what they were created to be, he finds them disobedient, self-seeking, refusing to give honour where honour belongs, in short, guilty. Such is the righteousness of God that such guilt cannot go unpunished, not if God is to remain God. Punishment is therefore meted out in just measure, taking the form of an infinite variety of unpleasantnesses but specifically including the ultimate frustration of human ambitions, and, finally, the death penalty. Men can have no ground for complaint: they have deserved what they get. If they complain that they can see no correlation between the crime and the punishment, this is simply to be interpreted as a further sign of guilt, rebelliousness which refuses to submit to the necessary judgment of God.

That such a picture is a caricature of anything that Christians understand by the righteousness of God should be obvious enough. But it can all too easily emerge – with all its nightmare results of guilt and lovelessness and terror – if our understanding of God's righteousness is not integrated into our understanding of his love. God is righteous, he is to be feared, judgment is a reality, but not because he is a cold, all-knowing 'meter-out-of-justice', but because he is love. In terms of human experience, the man most conscious of the righteousness of God, and so of his own sin, is not the unforgiven sinner but the love-reflecting saint.

2.2 Righteousness and love are not to be separated – that is certainly the theme of the biblical witness. It is an ancient heresy that the God of the Old Testament is a God of vengeance, while the God of the New Testament is a God of love, and it is a heresy because in the Old Testament there is no evidence to support this interpretation. Certainly there are many 'hard sayings', prophesies of impending doom, punishments for individual and national sin; 'vengeance is mine and recompense' (Deut. 32.35); 'the fear of the Lord is the beginning of wisdom' (Ps. 111.10). But it is often forgotten that the New Testament has its 'hard sayings' too: the visions of the trials of 'the last days' (Matt. 24; Mark 13; Luke 21), the parables of judgment, especially the Last Judgment (Matt. 25.31–46): 'unless you repent, you will all of you come to the same end' (Luke 13.5). But the important feature of both Testaments' references to God's righteousness and the consequences for mankind of his righteousness is that it is known and proclaimed in the light of his mercy, his love.

2.2.1 In the Old Testament, where the word translated 'righteousness' can mean also 'straightness', 'justice', 'right', 'justness', 'honesty', it is always used of God as a reflection of his goodness. He is righteous in that he is true to himself, self-consistent, and can be relied on to do what is right, what is consistent with himself. The word does not only, or even primarily, refer to punishment of the wicked or the disobedient. It is a pointer to his mercy, to his generosity to the needy, his pity for the suffering and the helpless, his faithfulness to those to whom he has committed himself. Thus to 'claim God's righteousness' is not so much to call down disaster on men's enemies as to claim God's forgiveness. When God asserts his righteousness, he asserts not his destructive power but his purpose of salvation. Understandably, there is in the Old Testament the closest connection between the righteousness of God and the covenant relationship with him into which Israel understood itself to have been called. He is known to be righteous because he has communicated his promises to Israel and proved his faithfulness. Conversely, it is within the covenant that Israel discovers a standard for judging its own behaviour, for exposing faithlessness, disobedience, any behaviour which is inconsistent with that required of a covenant people. It is in the context of the covenant that Israelites discover 'we are all as an unclean thing, and all our righteousnesses are as filthy rags' (Isa. 64.6). It is only because of this faith in the covenant, in God's promises, that Israel could take the quite astonishing step of interpreting national disaster as divine justice, and reach the incredible conclusion: 'Blessed is the man whom thou chastenest, O God, and teachest him out of thy law' (Ps. 94.12). God's righteousness and his reaction to infringement of it is not understood as something God has to do to protect his honour, as it were. It is understood rather in the sense of his determination that nothing less than his purpose of love for his creatures will be achieved, in the sense that he will not cease to be himself.

2.2.2 This is all summed up in the unequivocal New Testament statement that it is in the Gospel of Christ that the righteousness of God is revealed from faith to faith (Rom. 1.17). It has already been insisted that the Christian view of reality is based on the understanding that Jesus is not merely the teacher or the example of God's love: in him, God's love takes the form of a life lived. But the effect of this is not to leave God's righteousness and justice in a suspended, qualified or equivocal state. It certainly does not mean that sin does not really matter after all. It was in fact for, because of and by human sinfulness that Jesus was rejected and put to death. The New Testament will not let us forget about judgment and condemnation any more than the Old. On the contrary, these aspects of God's righteousness are made known precisely at the point where his love is lived – in Jesus Christ.

2.3 God loves, then, without ceasing to be righteous; he is just, without ceasing to be love. What, then, of what is traditionally known as his wrath and of the 'fear of the Lord'? As regards wrath, it has to be said that there is no hidden depth of experience or far country of despair where the identifying, accepting love of God cannot, indeed, has not reached, where reality, his reality, is not waiting to be known. But his love is not tyrannical. No one can be forced into recognizing it, which is to respond to it in love. To refuse to recognize reality, his reality, is to miss the point of life, the opportunity of sharing in the divine love. The consequences may well not be physically painful or mentally disruptive. There is no evidence that they are necessarily dramatic. But the consequences are a life of delusion, of ultimate opting out, of final failure. Saying 'No' to the divine love (and so to other people) is self-inflicted banishment from life, is choosing to remain finally closed in on oneself in ultimate separation – that is the wrath of God.

2.4 Is there, then, no room for 'the fear of the Lord' which the Psalmist designates as 'the beginning of wisdom' and which was such a popular theme for preachers in an earlier age? It is mercifully true that hell-fire and brimstone sermonic extravaganzas are a rarity now. They have been exposed as a very odd way of commending the Gospel: God is such that people are not to be frightened into a faith that is real. The fear of the Lord is not fear of discomfort or physical pain or natural disaster. Nor is it fear in face of the totally unknown. These are both natural and legitimate kinds of fear, but they are not fear of the Lord. The fear of the Lord is not illusory, but it is the fear of being loved totally, the compound of personal unworthiness, mystery and the abandonment of false security which the challenge of perfect love brings. T. S. Eliot expresses it in a profound and beautiful way in a prayer:

> Forgive us, O Lord, we acknowledge ourselves
>   as type of the common man,
> Of the men and women who shut the door
>   and sit by the fire;
> Who fear the blessing of God, the loneliness
>   of the night of God, the surrender required,
>   the deprivation inflicted;
> Who fear the injustice of men less than the
>   justice of God;
> Who fear the hand at the window, the fire
>   in the thatch, the fist in the tavern,
>   the push into the canal
> Less than we fear the love of God.[2]

107

The fear of the Lord is real, but it is fear not of divine punishment but of divine love.

3 In most men's minds, there is a natural association between righteousness and both freedom and power. Perfect righteousness presupposes freedom to make a perfect judgment and power to exercise it. We therefore consider next what can be said of God's freedom and then of his power.

Just as we had to insist that God's righteousness could only be spoken of in the light of his love, so now we must say that it is in the light of his love that his *freedom* is to be grasped. As the greatest of contemporary theologians, Karl Barth, has put it: God is 'the One who loves in freedom'.[3] We have already seen that God's love is a liberating love, and we discussed briefly the kind of freedom into which it liberated men. Now we have to say what is meant when we say God is free.

3.1 It means first of all that he is free to be himself. Perhaps this sounds too obvious to need stating, but this is something on which traditional theology, with its doctrines of the divine immutability, impassibility and so on has placed great, probably too great emphasis. The main point behind this emphasis was the insight, which we can still share to some extent, that no external circumstance or power, nothing that is not God can force him to be other than he is, can exercise any constraint on him, can impose any obligation on him. He is free from all conditioning or determination from without by that which is not himself. In this way, it was thought to protect the independence of God from his creation; he is not the sum total of human values and hopes and aspirations: creation needs him but the relation is not reciprocal, he would be himself without creation.

3.2 This is, however, a dangerous line of argument, which can only be followed to the end by ignoring the data and separating freedom from love. God is free to be himself. But if we are not going to turn our backs on everything that has been said about the love of God, then great care must be taken not to set up 'freedom' in competition with 'love'. It is as perfect love that God is free; if he ceases to be perfect love he ceases to be himself. How do we know? His commitment to and involvement and identification with his creatures and his creation is the pledge that he can be absolutely and eternally relied on not to 'lose interest', as we might put it, or to cease to be himself.

3.3 Perhaps a brief data check might help to elucidate the freedom of perfect love. If we look to the life of Jesus as it is presented in the Gospels, it is possible to see that he was under no external compulsion to love sinners, to identify himself with them. Nothing forced him to act in the way that he did and to invite the consequences of his actions. He chose to do so. In theory, it would have been possible for him at any time to halt on the path of obedience to the Father, at some point to stop short of total self-giving. But the faith of the whole Church in all ages is based on the fact that he did not halt or turn back. Such was his freedom, to be open to all the world, to love without reserve.

So, too, in our own limited experience. When we act in love, it is true that there is a sense in which we act under compulsion. 'We can't help it'. But the experience itself is the very opposite of constraint: we know of no other situation in which we are more truly free.

4 God, then, is free to be himself. He is also free to act as he wills, to accomplish what he wills. It would be a real qualification of his freedom if we had to admit that, though he might want or will certain things, he was unable to bring them about through lack of power, or knowledge. It is in order to rule out this possibility that theology has introduced all the 'omni-' words – omnipotent ('almighty'), omniscient, omnipresent, omnivolent etc. – which many people find utterly perplexing, if not embarrassing. The embarrassment arises because the mere occurrence of tragedies or disasters or injustices – and let no one claim that these are illusory – seems a denial either of God's goodness or his power. Why does he allow it to happen? Either he has not the power to prevent it, even if he has the desire, or he lacks the desire, even if he has the power. Are we not then simply asking for trouble by even trying to show that these 'omni-' words still have meaning? Our contention is that they can be meaningful, but only if they are considered against the background of God's love.

4.1 As a first example we consider what is meant by the omnipotence of God. He is spoken of as all-powerful, he is worshipped and praised by Christians as 'Almighty'. What sort of power, of might, is referred to here? Our age is predisposed to think of power in physical terms. The word brings to mind the end-product of an atomic generating station, or the roar of the racing car or the jumbo-jet. But other kinds of power spring readily to mind: the power of the financier with his silent, undramatic but effective dealings influencing the lives of many; the power of the dictator, political or criminal, with his hoodlums at his side, ready to draw and fire at his nod. There are still other forms of power, more elusive but none the less real because they are the power of ideas coming to the surface and ideals coming into sight from a particular vantage point. So in the 1960's we have witnessed in turn 'Flower Power', 'Black Power', 'Student Power', all offering convincing proof in their different ways of the power of ideas to change people's lives and to get things done, all proving in their own way that words are not without power, even suggesting that in an age when there is more available physical power than ever before, the pen may yet be mightier than the sword. But still we have not exhausted our catalogue of power. This would have to include such divergent things as the suggestive power of a song – 'We shall overcome', perhaps – or the hidden persuasion of the advertiser, the dynamism of group behaviour. All this is simple enough, but there is yet one kind of power so obvious that it is easily overlooked, and that is the power of love.

It is not really being sentimental to say that in human terms of getting things done, there is no greater power than love. There is no need to exaggerate here or pretend that love is the only thing that gets things done. Terror can make

110

a man do much, duty can make a man do more; financial incentives can accomplish a great deal, as can simple pride, backed by the fear of failure or being found out. But the simple fact, endorsed by human experience, is that love enables a man freely and willingly to go beyond anything that fear or duty, incentive bonuses or pride could ever make possible, beyond anything the man himself or anyone else could expect of him. In the words of St Paul: 'There is nothing love cannot face; there is no limit to its faith, its hope and its endurance' (I Cor. 13.7).

4.2 The power of God is the power of divine love. It is omnipotence because it is adequate to his purpose, and his purpose is to make his love available. This gives us the clue to the solution of two problems which naturally arise whenever God's omnipotence is asserted: Why then does he not interfere? How does he exercise his power?

4.2.1 If he is omnipotent, why does he not interfere? The situation we have in mind is the situation of suffering, personal or corporate: a baby is born with some incurable disease; a child is maimed for life in a road accident; a whole village is destroyed by an earthquake; a whole country is reduced to starvation by drought. If God is love, how can he want this to happen? If he is all-powerful, how can he allow it to happen? In trying to answer these questions, great sensitivity is demanded and a total absence of callousness, coupled with a readiness to admit that there is much that we do not know and no question of our pretending to see the whys and wherefores of every situation. But it is nevertheless possible to see on reflection that if God's power is the power of love, it cannot be part of his purpose to over-ride human freedom (e.g. by forcing the driver of the car to put his brake on, or by God's intervening himself or forcing men to irrigate drought-prone territories). Nor can it be part of his purpose to prevent nature acting naturally when human lives or welfare are threatened. If his power is the power of love, then the test of his omnipotence is not whether accidents occur, or tragedies or disasters, but whether there is any circumstance or situation in which his love is not active, in which it cannot be known and responded to. In the Christian understanding of reality and, indeed, the Christian experience of reality, there is no such situation. At all times, however hopeless, loveless or black, God is there, on the side of the sufferer, in identifying love, introducing for the sufferer a creative possibility of responding love, of life, even in the face of death. The great biblical texts of the divine ability, summed up in the famous ascription of praise, 'Now to Him who is able to do immeasurably more than all we can ask or conceive, by the power which is at work among us' (Eph. 3.20. See also Heb. 7.25; Mark 10.27), are not appropriated and repeated by Christians in defiance of all the evidence, or because 'the Bible says so'. They reflect what Christians have discovered to be true.

4.2.2 The reference to 'the power which is at work among us' brings us to the second question: If God is all-powerful, how does he exercise his power? Here again it must be insisted that he does not exert his power by over-riding human freedom (with all the consequences, good or bad, which that implies) or intervening to change God-given natural conditions of life in this universe. His power is the power of love, and as love begets love, he achieves his purpose by allowing men to respond to and so to share in his love.

This may be put another way. Things get done in the world or fail to get done because of the actions of men. Purposes are fulfilled or frustrated by what men do. What they do depends, in the last resort, on who they are, what they consider to be important, really real. God exercises his power – we may even use the word control – not by force but by love, by presenting himself to men in such a way that in the exercise of their freedom they can (but not must) respond, and the only true way of response is a response of love. In this way, God, without in the least infringing upon human freedom, enables people to become different people, to pursue the purposes of love, to do what love requires to be done. This is how he exercises his power, by making it possible for those who respond to him to share it. The love of God in Christ both makes all things 'new' (II Cor. 5.17; Rev. 21.5) and makes it possible for a man to say without hyperbole yet without a hint of the fantasy-world of Batman and Superman: 'I have strength for anything through him who gives me power' (Phil. 4.13).

4.3 As we pass from omnipotence to another 'omni'-word, omniscience, we are really simply drawing out the implications of omnipotence, of God's being able to achieve his ends. For ability demands knowledge, and in speaking of God's omniscience, we are confessing that God's knowledge is in some sense equal to its objects both actual and potential, both of what is and of what is possible.

4.3.1 In the last chapter (see pp. 87 f.), it was claimed that the divine knowledge is not that of the detached outside observer. It was, rather, 'inside' knowledge, of one who knows the situation from the inside and whose motive is love. This rules out the possibility that the divine knowledge is in any way comparable to that of a 'Big Brother', spying on everything that goes on in order to pounce on any irregularity and put a decisive stop to any dangerous or unwelcome development. It is rather the knowledge of love, the untyrannical knowledge of complete sensitivity to everything that is, to everything that happens and to everything that can happen, to actualities and potentialities in all creation.

4.3.2 We have already seen that although such knowledge is complete, extending to what has happened, what is happening and what will happen, because it is bound up with love it does not in any way imply the denial of human freedom. It does not imply determinism, or mean that the choices we make are not real choices. They are real choices, they are not determined in advance, we are free to opt for one thing or one course of action rather than another and this freedom of choice is not illusory. But the divine omniscience does mean that God knows us and all that exists so well that he knows what choice in given circumstances we will go for. Such is his love that he presents himself to us in

113

such a way as to set before us the possibility of choosing to act in love, of making his purpose ours. The most useful analogy here is the parent–child relationship or the counsellor–client situation. Good parents know how their child will react in a given situation: the good counsellor knows what possibilities are available to the person he is trying to help. But such knowledge is not normally neutral information picked up by superior intelligence. It is rather acquired by intimate acquaintance with the child or the client, with imaginative insight into the situation mediated by sensitivity. It does not force the child to act in a certain way or make the client opt for one possibility rather than another; their freedom is not prejudiced. But parental love in the one case and concern in the other has penetrated the darkness of the situation, and may even make possible additional choices that would not otherwise be available. So, too, the divine knowledge is no impersonal affair of machine-like efficiency. It is inseparably bound up with love. It can justifiably be called omniscience because it is grounded in the total, universal nature of God's love.

4.4 Of that other 'omni-' word, 'omnipresence', we need say little at this point, as we have in effect discussed it earlier (see pp. 70 ff.). To describe God as omnipresent is neither overbelief nor 'extrapolation to the skies', because it is a necessary feature of his freedom and so of his love. If he really does will to give himself in love to his creatures, if he really is related to everything that is, if his purpose of love is not to be fragmentary or partial, then he must be free to be present everywhere and at all times without ceasing to be himself. He must be free to provide ever new possibilities of response. That he is present everywhere and at all times is then the presupposition of his love, and the corollary of this is that there is literally no situation conceivable in which he may not be responded to and known.

5 The reference to God's being present to his creation without ceasing to be himself suggests some reference to the mystery of God, and in particular his holiness. For holiness has traditionally been used to refer to the 'Wholly Otherness' of God. Man and his world are creatures, between whom and God there is an 'infinite qualitative difference', in Søren Kierkegaard's famous phrase. Even when God gives himself to his creatures and so is not 'Wholly Other', he is free to remain himself, his 'Wholly Otherness' is in no sense diminished. Indeed, when he communicates, what is made known is the One who is wholly Other, in his love, righteousness and freedom transcending our love, righteousness and freedom. Even when he holds communion with his creatures he retains that transcendent love, righteousness, freedom, so that even in the moment of communion, the only appropriate initial response is that of the prophet Isaiah: 'Woe is me! for I am undone' (Isa. 6.5); or of Simon Peter in the presence of Jesus: 'Go, Lord, leave me, sinner that I am!' (Luke 5.8). It is, then, not without reason that holiness has been called the sheer, incommensurate God-ness of God, or 'the consummate glory of all the divine perfections in union'.[4]

As such, it might be argued that the holiness of God should have been discussed right at the start of our attempt to answer the question 'Who is God?' But we have preferred to withhold consideration of this subject until this point not because it is in any way subsidiary or unimportant but because the holiness we wish to speak of is not any kind of holiness or holiness in the abstract but specifically the holiness of God who is love.

5.1 It has been claimed that holiness is the distinctive religious category, the 'shudder-making' property, the mystery, the 'numinous' which invades human experience and gives rise to the feeling of dread and the emotion of awe.[5] It is more than wisdom, and therefore non-rational, and more than goodness, and therefore non-moral, but it gives religion its essential quality. Religious advance, on this view, would consist in an ever-increasing association of this element with reason and morality, and in Christianity it is perfectly rationalized and ethicized. This way of looking at holiness is helpful and realistic in that it brings out the total otherness of God, the fact that he is not to be exhaustively comprehended by human minds, far less totally understood in terms of intellectual truth or moral perfection. But it is deficient on at least two counts.

5.1.1 In the first place, while it is undoubtedly true that in the history of religions, the unknown, the beyond has frequently been identified as something like the numinous, and experienced in a response of awe or dread, it would be difficult to say that such is always the case. Many men and women in the Western world today could not endorse this experience. Certainly, a kind of dread in the face of the unknown does seem to be the universal experience of mankind, but it is dread in the face of ignorance, or in the face of meaninglessness or pointlessness, not dread before something that is experienced as 'eerie'. 'Eeriness' implies 'spookiness', and for most of us now this belongs to the entertainment world of ghost stories and thrillers rather than the world of everyday life.

5.1.2 But in the second place, this view of holiness fails to do justice to the Christian understanding of reality. 'Spookiness' is a degenerate form of religion, not the norm of authentic faith. For God gives himself to be known as the sole reality worthy of worship not by demanding a response of dread or of hopeless fear in the face of the unknown, or even a response of awe in the sense of a trembling in ignorance and guilt. On the contrary, the final response which his holiness evokes and which is appropriate to it is the response of reverence in love.

5.2 It is curious that in the Bible, the word 'holy' is applied more often to men than to God. Indeed the New Testament name for Christians is sometimes 'saints', which literally means 'the holy ones'. The reason for this is not that men have suddenly become competitors to God in holiness. Rather is it taken for granted that men are only made holy when they are given in their lives of faith to reflect the holiness of God; not of course, by mere confession or ritual, but in responding with their whole lives to reality, by finding God in their neighbour, by active participation in his love.

6 To praise God is to glorify him, to acknowledge his glory. If holiness is a specifically religious category, 'glory' is not. It is a word much beloved of the advertising industry and indispensable to the tourist trade. It carries powerful associations, the spectacularly beautiful, the highly colourful, not to say garish, that which is to be revelled in, admired and enjoyed ('that glorious feeling'!). Despite its debasement at the hands of popular culture, it still retains something of its original associations of dignity, worthy of honour, and this is why Christians find it still appropriate to use it of God.

6.1 In its original use, glory is something like the honour or respect owed to sheer size, or worth, or ownership of property, the dignity which is attested by gorgeous apparel, radiant appearance and so on. When the Old Testament applies it to God, it usually indicates his dignity, his right both to maintain and declare it, almost to make himself conspicuous as the one he is. It is thus associated with the more spectacular effects of nature, with visual symbols of brilliance, blinding light before which men can but veil their faces. In the New Testament, glory is concentrated not so much on the spectacular effects of God's presence and action but on his very presence and action itself: all thought of glory is concentrated on Jesus Christ as the one who is and can be known as the triumph of God's freedom and love.

6.2 It is this note of triumph which ultimately justifies our confession of God as glorious and to be glorified. That his purposes are vindicated, that nothing can come between him and their fulfilment, that all that threatens can never have the last word – these clear notes of triumph refuse to be silenced.

The hope that lies before those who know the reality of God is so invincible, so triumphant, that it is both liberating and resolute, both martyr-making and tyrant-breaking. This accent of triumph in God's glory makes it possible to speak of beauty – without some notion of glory, the 'beauty of holiness', for example, could be but a cool, subdued and dim affair. But it also makes it possible to speak of joy, that quality significant by its absence from so many contemporary expressions of Christian faith. The joy here referred to is not the cheery chumminess characteristic of certain brands of piety, the synthetic smile, the ostentatious chirpiness that knows all the answers by being insensitive to all the problems. Rather the joy here intended is that born of the underlying confidence of those who have discovered that the glory of ultimate reality is not of decorative splendour or naked, alien power, but of the God who is love, and who is on our side.

NOTES

1. Bishop Pike, quoted in *Time Magazine*, November 11, 1966.

2. T. S. Eliot, *Murder in the Cathedral* (London: Faber and Faber, 1936), p. 85. Quoted by permission.

3. Karl Barth, *Church Dogmatics* II 1 (English translation, Edinburgh: T. and T. Clark, 1957), section 28.

4. By H. H. Farmer and H. H. Hodge respectively.

5. Rudolf Otto, *The Idea of the Holy* (English Translation, London: Humphrey Milford, 1923).

7 Postscript—Unfinished Business

We have come to the end of our study, conscious of the many, many things that might have been said but have not been said in our attempt to answer the question at issue. Our task, however, was not to give a resumé of the whole of Christian doctrine but rather to give some indication of what Christians are doing when they use the word 'God'. Yet it might be helpful if we now try to underline all that we have been saying with a single-phrase definition.

Who is God? From the start, the data would not allow us to rest content with any definition which converted the 'who' into a 'what', an impersonal, thing-like substance. We therefore rejected as positively a misleading emphasis the Westminster Shorter Catechism's answer: 'God is a Spirit, infinite, eternal and unchangeable in His being, wisdom, power, holiness, justice, goodness and truth'. It might have been possible to settle for 'Ultimate Reality', 'the Really Real', or 'What ultimately matters', but here again while such a definition would be accurate in so far as it implies the total, ultimate involvement of everything that is, it fails to indicate unequivocally the personal element which we have seen to be so important. On the other hand, a definition such as 'personality controlled by will', while successfully avoiding impersonal associations, fails to convey the absolute relatedness to God to everything that exists. Perhaps the definition which best fits all we have been trying to say and most readily makes way for an understanding of God in terms of love is this: *God is he with whom we have to do.*

This definition is, of course, formal: it does not say much about God, it requires to be filled up with content. But it does have certain advantages over the other definitions we have mentioned. To begin with, it stresses the utterly personal nature of God – and we tried to show what 'personal' in this context means as well as how certain 'qualifiers' might be used of God to prevent him being thought of as just one person among many. Further, it indicates the self-involving nature of our language about God: when we speak of God, we are not speaking about some alien thing or third party with whom we may, if we so choose, have some dealings. We are speaking about him to whom we and everything that exists is, by the very fact of existence, necessarily related, whether we know it or not, whether we like it or not. Again, such a definition suggests that it is not in talking but in being and living that we have to do with God, a matter of whole life. Finally, such a definition offers an appropriate conceptual framework for the gospel or good news of who he is: He with whom we have to do is none other than he who has to do with us in love and freedom, who has declared his purpose and given himself in Jesus Christ, the flesh and blood invitation to acknowledge the secret of God's being and of man's *raison d'être* as love.

Neither the definition nor the gospel can provide all the answers. Just as the scientist acknowledges that there is always far more to learn about his particular subject than the accumulated study of the centuries has yet revealed, so the theologian freely acknowledges that when he has said all he can say of God, the mystery remains. It is not incumbent on the Christian, therefore, to provide a reason for everything that happens, or a prediction of everything that will happen in the future, before or after death. On the contrary, he denies the knowledge of reality he professes if he pretends that he sees the answer to every question posed to the mind of man, for his place in reality is not the mastermind, the collector and purveyor of knowledge, but the active participant in love. He knows that the one God who identifies himself with humanity in Jesus is the same God who is active in all creation, furthering his purpose by providing the possibilities open to the world of nature and to men of every age and creed. So the Christian is never afraid to change his mind, ever open to new insights, however unlikely the source. Marx and Darwin, for example, were no orthodox believers, but both have provided invaluable motives to Christians to probe more deeply their understanding of God's activity in the created world, in human communities, and of the disruptive effects of sin.

Knowledge of who God is, therefore, is not omniscience. Far from inhibiting or putting a brake on enquiry into every aspect of the natural and human world, it provides the motivation for just such an enquiry. If to know God is to be given the freedom to see participation in his love as the purpose of life, then the motivation now is not to satisfy curiosity, or knowledge for knowledge's sake, but to find a more complete expression of love, with great imagination to discover the new possibilities of love that lie before us. Love makes every man a scientist in his own way.

Even more important, knowledge of who God is binds every man to his neighbour in a new, essential way. It frees us for our fellow man near or far, for without him we cannot know ourselves or respond in love to the divine reality. There is indeed much that the Christian does not know, but the one thing he knows with the certainty of faith, verifiable only in life, is that by identifying himself with us and for us in Jesus, God has declared that it is in living for others that the purpose of our life is to be realized.

To know who God is is to be committed to his purpose, and to be committed to his purpose is to be committed to others. This means, negatively, that for the Christian there is no false optimism. He cannot opt out of the world of others into a fantasy world of self-isolation, however piously intended. He is wholly involved in that world of others with its tragedies as well as its triumphs, its failures and its crime and shame as well as its achievements and joys. This also means positively, that in this world of others, he brings his knowledge of Christ, the really real, whom he discovers waiting before him in the creative opportunity of love which lies in every situation which is or can ever be. That is enough for consistent (though not unchanging) action on the basis of what we know. That is enough for openness to what we do not yet know, to the future that lies ahead. That is enough, for hope that can never, literally never, be shaken, for life that is more abundant, for entry into the joy of the Lord.

> It is not to be thought that I have already achieved all this. I have not yet reached perfection, but I press on, hoping to take hold of that for which Christ once took hold of me. My friends, I do not reckon myself to have got hold of it yet. All I can say is this: forgetting what is behind me, and reaching out for that which lies ahead, I press towards the goal to win the prize which is God's call to the life above, in Christ Jesus. Let us then keep to this way of thinking, those of us who are mature. If there is any point on which you think differently, this also God will make plain to you. Only let our conduct be consistent with the level we have already reached. (Phil. 3.12–16)

Suggestions for Further Reading

Baelz, P. R., *Christian Theology and Metaphysics*, Epworth Press, 1968

Baillie, John, *The Sense of the Presence of God*, OUP, 1962

Bowden, J. & Richmond, J. (Eds.), *A Reader in Contemporary Theology*, SCM Press and Westminster Press, 1967

Flew, Antony, *God and Philosophy*, Hutchinson and Harcourt, Brace & World, 1966

Flew, A. & MacIntyre, A. (Eds.), *New Essays in Philosophical Theology*, SCM Press and The Macmillan Co., 1955

Haroutunian, Joseph, *God with Us*, Epworth Press and Westminster Press, 1967

Hick, John, *Philosophy of Religion*, Prentice-Hall Inc., 1964

Jenkins, D. E., *Guide to the Debate about God*, Lutterworth Press and Westminster Press, 1966

McIntyre, John, *On the Love of God*, Collins and Harper & Row, 1962

Ogden, Schubert, *The Reality of God, and Other Essays*, SCM Press and Harper & Row, 1967

Ogletree, T. W., *The 'Death of God' Controversy*, SCM Press and Abingdon Press, 1966

Ramsey, Ian T., *Religious Language*, SCM Press and The Macmillan Co., 1957

Robinson, J. A. T., *Exploration into God*, SCM Press and Stanford University Press, 1967

Smith, R. Gregor, *Secular Christianity*, Collins and Harper & Row, 1966

Taylor, A. E., *Does God Exist?*, Collins Fontana Books, 1961

Tillich, Paul, *Biblical Religion and the Search for Ultimate Reality*, James Nisbet, 1956 and University of Chicago Press, 1955

Walsh, W. H., *Metaphysics*, Hutchinson and Hillary House, 1963

and a classic

Hume, David, *Dialogue Concerning Natural Religion*, 1779

Index